Communicating with Microcomputers

by

Ian Cullimore

Sigma Press • Wilmslow

First published in 1987
Reprinted 1988

Sigma Press
98a Water Lane, Wilmslow, SK9 5BB, England.

ISBN 1-85058-055-3

Typeset by
Minstrel
Dane Road, Sale, M33 2BY, England.

Printed and bound in Great Britain
at The Camelot Press plc, Southampton

British Library Cataloguing in Publication Data

Cullimore, Ian
Communicating with microcomputers.
1. Microcomputer 2. Computer interfaces
I. Title
004.6'16   TK7888.3

Distributed by
John Wiley & Sons Ltd., Baffins Lane, Chichester, West Sussex, England.

Preface

Communicating with microcomputers seems to be the flavour of the year. Gone from people's attention are last year's fads of spreadsheets, wordprocessors, and integrated packages. Now the talk is of connecting microcomputers to printers, "dumping" files from one microcomputer to another, and even connecting many computers together in a "network".

It is remarkable, therefore, just how difficult and perplexing it generally proves to be for the layman, and even the experienced professional, to cope with the standards and systems imposed on him in trying to communicate in practice. This is perhaps a result of the fact that communications standards and ideas have been passed down from researchers of many years ago without the end-user in mind; indeed, before the end-user or even the term "end-user" was around. The situation has not been helped by the fact that different manufacturers have chosen to interpret the standards set down in different ways, creating a non-standard "standard" system!

This book aims to try to unravel some of these mysteries, and guide the inexperienced and experienced alike through some of the mazes which have arisen on the way to a fuller understanding of communications. Of course, different people will probably want different things out of the book — some will be looking for an overall knowledge of the subject, some may well be developing software communications projects themselves, whilst others (and perhaps the majority), will simply be struggling to get their microcomputer to print something — anything! — out onto paper.

The book starts with a consideration of overall standards in communications, and how these should be determined. Thus the subject of *character sets* and *representation of data* will also be considered.

Chapter 2 starts to formalize our abstract ideas of communications into concrete examples — although still of a largely theoretical nature — of data transmission.

In Chapter 3 a full consideration is made of the most widely used interface standard — the *RS-232*. This leads naturally, in Chapter 4, onto the practicalities of data communication using the RS-232, and some newer standards based on it: *RS-449*, *RS-423* and *RS-422*. Finally, the subject is rounded off in Chapter 5 with a consideration of *handshaking*: how to control the flow of data between communicating devices.

Chapter 6 takes a break from the nitty-gritty of exact communications standards, and looks at the subject of *terminal emulation*; Chapter 7, meanwhile, is not one for the faint-hearted, as the subject of actually writing a communications package, both in a *high-level language*, and *assembly language*, is given some careful and deep consideration.

To round off the subject of the RS-232 and its applications, Chapter 8 looks into how computers talk to the outside world via the telephone network, using *modems* and *acoustic couplers*.

Until this point, the type of communications considered has been largely centred around the RS-232, and has thus been of a *serial* nature. However, Chapter 9 concerns itself with an alternative method — *parallel* communications — and two widely-used industry standards: the *Centronics* interface and the *IEEE 488* interface.

Chapter 10 moves onto a topic much in the news nowadays (at least in the computing industry!) — *Local Area Networks*, whilst Chapters 11 and 12 concern themselves with the very important, and very large, topic of *file transfer*.

A break is taken from conventional computer communications systems with a look, in Chapter 13, at the *Musical Instrument Digital Interface* — computers playing music!

In Chapters 14 through to 16, we look at two very popular communications packages for the IBM PC — one available from the IBM PC User Group called *Kermit*, the other Microstuf Inc's *Crosstalk* — and the ever-expanding topic of *Electronic Mail*, with a look at British Telecom's service, *Telecom Gold*.

Finally, Chapter 17 takes a look at how, in practice, to successfully wire up RS-232 interfaces from one device to another, with a consideration of some everyday machines like the IBM PC.

For those interested in the topic, Appendix I is a table of the ASCII character set, and Appendix II is a similar table of IBM's equivalent for its mainframe computers — the EBCDIC character set.

CONTENTS

CHAPTER 1

Communications Standards –An Overview

This book is all about how to make the often elegant, but usually quite dumb, microcomputer on your desktop actually communicate with the outside world. This may simply be, as is most often the case, a desire to produce a listing of your latest program, sales report for your masters, or a copy of your latest literary masterpiece. Or it may be necessary to transfer a file of data from one computer to another. If they are of the same type, or compatible in that they will accept ("read") the same format and size of floppy disk, then this will be straight forward. However, this is not usually the case. Often as not, you will have a vital file, once lovingly created at great expense of time and effort, saved on a disk somewhere. This may be a file created in a database package, or a document created by using a word processor. Whatever the case, you may find yourself with a redundant computer system, or caught in the middle of a system "upgrade" . The alternative course, of manually typing in your precious files, is surely not very appealling!

What is required to effect a successful transfer of your files from the old to the new is some system of reading the file to be transfered character by character, and transmitting these by some process (as yet unspecified!) to the receiving computer, whereupon this latter computer will understand what it is receiving, and hence save your transmitted characters, one by one, in some place of safety.

Even more exciting is the possibility of "downloading" your file of data, perhaps across the telephone lines using a modem link, into an unknown, and possibly unseen, computer system, to be accessed later by colleagues. And all in a matter of seconds!

1.1 The Need to Specify a Standard

In this instance, the two computers or devices in question will have to communicate, or "talk" to each other. How is this to be achieved? A common standard for a system of talking will obviously have to be agreed on – the computers will have to talk the same language if they are to understand one another. Let us consider the sort of things that have to be decided:

How are these characters to be specified and translated?

How are these translated characters to be transmitted?

How will the receiving computer know to expect a character?

How will the receiving computer know when a character starts, and when it stops? And how will it know when the whole file has been transmitted?

How, too, can computers tell each other when to slow down or stop, and when to start transmitting again?

As will be seen in the following chapters, there is of course no unique solution to these questions – after all, we human beings talk in more than one language! There are many different solutions, each of which try to cater for different problems and criteria. However, out of the numerous possibilities, at least some common and widespread standards have arisen. There is, perhaps, some hope.

1.2 Character sets

Any discussion of character sets must, perhaps unfortunately for some who may be put off the idea, be preceded by some sort of explanation of the internal workings of a computer, and how characters are to be internally represented.

Almost all computers nowadays work on the principle of using groups of binary digits, or "bits", to represent data. Each bit may be a 1 or a 0. This stems from the nature of the electronics used in microprocessors – only two states are possible: off and on, or high and low, or logical true or false. Furthermore, most microprocessors group these bits together into a string of eight, called a "byte".

Thus, as examples of bytes we have (in so-called binary representation):

a)   10110011

b)   11111111

c)   00000000

d)   00110001

Now, in the binary representation, the groups of 8 bits are represented by a binary number. In a binary number system, as with a number system using any base (such as our normal base 10 system, or even a number system using a base of 8, or 16, for instance), a number is expressed in ascending powers of its base, which is in this case 2.

Thus the binary number

hgfedcba,

where h, g, ... ,a are 0 or 1, is

a times 2 to the power of 0

plus b times 2 to the power of 1

plus c times 2 to the power of 2

plus d times 2 to the power of 3

plus e times 2 to the power of 4

plus f times 2 to the power of 5

plus g times 2 to the power of 6

plus h times 2 to the power of 7.

So in our example a) above,

10110011

we have

a=1+2+16+32+128

Similarly, b=255 (decimal), and c=0.

A more convenient way to represent such numbers and bytes, especially when dealing with computers, is using the hexadecimal representation. This means using a number system to the base 16. Now, a byte can be split into two half-bytes, or "nibbles", by grouping the eight bits into two sets of four bits each, called (appropriately enough), the high nibble and low nibble. A nibble is half a byte!

Consider again

10110011

We can alternatively represent this:

1011 0011

It just so happens that each nibble has a range of values from 0 to $1+2+4+8$, i.e. from 0 to 15. So using a number system based on powers of 16, each nibble can be represented by a single digit. By convention, the hexadecimal digits are:

0 1 2 3 4 5 6 7 8 9 A B C D E F

where A is equivalent to 10 in our usual decimal system,
and   B is equivalent to 11,

and   C is equivalent to 12 etc.

Thus in our example above, (a) can be represented alternatively as:

   1+2+8 1+2

   i.e. B3

To avoid ambiguity, "(hex)" or just "H" is often written after a number expressed in hexadecimal, e.g B3H or B3 (hex).

This is surely a much more elegant, and compact, way of representing bytes!

1.3 The ASCII character set

Perhaps the most widely used and internationally agreed coding system, at least in the English speaking world, is the ASCII (American Standard Code for Information Interchange) Character Set, or Code.

Consider what is required to represent the English language: there are 26 letters, each of which can be upper or lower case, plus 10 numeric symbols, as well as various special characters such as ! $ and }.

Now, the letters and numbers require 62 characters so far; we could think of some two dozen more special characters in common usage, in addition.

In our byte system described so far, we have the possibility of 256 unique numbers, from 0 (00000000) up to 256 (11111111, or FF in hexadecimal), which is obviously plenty. In actual fact, we have easily enough scope with just seven bits – this gives us 128 possible codes.

We can now set about ordering our representations of characters in some, admittedly quite arbitrary, order. As long as everyone agrees on the same order, however, there will be no confusion. For instance, we might assign the numbers 0 to 9 the codes

   00000000 to 000010001

   i.e. 00 to 09 (hexadecimal).

Unfortunately this is not the standard that has been chosen! Instead, in the ASCII Code, the numbers 0 to 9 occupy the range 00110000 to 00111001, or 30H to 39H (remember that 30H means 30 in the hexadecimal notation). Similarly, the alphabetic characters are assigned their own unique code.

There is a description, by means of an ASCII Conversion Table, in Appendix I of how the scheme is arranged.

As will be seen, the various characters are lumped together in convenient groups. As described above, the numerals occupy the range 30H to 39H. The first 32 characters, i.e. 00H to 1FH, are reserved for the exclusive use of so-called *control codes*. These are used for, as you might well imagine, providing control information between computers. For instance, at 0DH we have the familiar carriage return code, i.e. the return key on your computer or typewriter keyboard. At 0AH we have Line Feed, and at 07H a code which, if received by a computer, tells it to make a beeping sound (BELL).

The alphabetic characters conveniently occupy two groups, contiguous within themselves. From 41H to 5AH we have the upper case letters, and then from 61H to 7AH the lower case letters. You will notice that there is a convenient constant gap of 20H, or 32 decimal, between an upper case letter and its lower case equivalent. This, as will be seen, is most convenient when translating from one to the other.

You may wonder if it is not wasteful using eight bits in a byte now, instead of the obvious seven that are all that are needed for our encoding system above. In fact, the spare eighth bit will turn out to be very useful later on, when considering how best to go about transmitting and receiving these characters with the minimum risk of anything going wrong.

The Extended ASCII Character Set

In actual fact, there is also an extension of the ASCII characterset which uses up all eight available bits. This is the character set used by, for instance, IBM for their desktop Personal Computer. Theextension of the character set thus allows for general compatibilitywith the non-extended ASCII character set, but also allows for foreign and unusual characters to be accessed easily.

1.4 IBM and the EBCDIC character set

IBM alone, amongst the major computer manufacturers, decided to specify their own coding system of representing alphanumeric data. But with their enormous industrial might, who was to argue with them?

The EBCDIC Code, which stands for Extended Binary Coded Decimal Interchange Code, is a variation on ASCII. It has two important features. Firstly, it uses the full eight bits of each byte. This obviously means that more characters can be included in the character set, in fact up to 256 as discussed previously. Second, the groups of both upper case and lower case letters are not contiguous. For instance, we have the group of letters A to I at C1H to C9H, and then J to R are at D1H to D9H. The numbers are at F0H to F9H. However, as with the ASCII Code, there is a constant difference between the upper and lower case letters, i.e. "a" is at 81H, and "A" is at C1H; "s" is at A2H, and "S" is at E2H, a difference of 40H or 64 decimal.

There is a complete description, by means of a conversion table, of the EBCDIC Code in Appendix II.

The EBCDIC Code, as specified by IBM, is generally peculiar only to their mainframe computers – their range of microcomputers, such as the PC, XT and AT, use the ASCII code system (in fact, Extended ASCII). This naturally helps enormously in providing compatibility between the vast range of microcomputers, printers and other devices on the market today.

1.5 Serial Transmission of Data

We have now set up our system of encoding characters uniquely into a byte. Let us use the ASCII Code for the remainder of this book by way of example.

We now have to consider ways of transmitting these bytes of data. Our first problem is the very nature of our system; each character is now in reality a string of eight bits. So for every character that needs transmitting, we have to actually transmit eight bits.

There is thus one crucial question that needs to be first answered: do we transmit these eight bits simultaneously, or in some sort of sequence? Let us consider the implications of either choice. If we choose the first option, to transmit the eight bits, and hence the complete byte and character code, simultaneously, then we have the advantage that the system will be fast; the whole character will be transmitted in one go.

Conversely, our second option of transmitting the individual bits of each byte one after the other, must necessarily be slower. However, it may prove in the long run to be more desirable. Consider the very mechanics of communication: simultaneous, or *parallel* transfer will require at a minimum one separate wire for each bit (since each bit will be, in electrical terms, either a 1 or a 0); however, our alternative *serial* transfer system will require only one wire for the transmission of the signal. This may prove to be advantageous.

1.6 Description of basic serial data transfer

Thus our idea is to transmit the constituent bytes one by one. How is this best achieved in practice? We know that our coding system is set up so that we have a binary system of ones and zeros; this can easily be translated, as we have said before, into plus and minus voltage signals on a wire. We can thus simply take our first bit of data, for instance the *rightmost* or *least significant* bit, and put this onto our transmit line. Then, after a pause, we place our next most significant bit on the line, and so forth until all our seven or eight bits are transmitted. Of course, we shall have to consider some more fundamental questions before our system can be made to operate in reality. For instance, how to warn the receiving computer that a character is on its way, how the receiving computer is to know that the last bit of data has been received, and so forth.

1.7 Parallel Transmission of Data

Our alternative idea, the parallel transfer of data, perhaps seems more straight forward. We obviously now need seven or eight separate pieces of wire (one for each bit – in some circumstances using the ASCII Code we may require only seven bits to be transfered), and our system will work such that each bit of data is placed onto its corresponding line simultaneously. As before, we shall still have to consider some fundamental questions, such as how to synchronize the whole affair so that the transmitting and receiving computers know when to expect to have to start and stop.

But the fundamentals of our complementary systems are now decided – all that has to be done is to universally agree on some standards, such as voltages, speeds, and even plugs and sockets, and the specification of a fully working system is within our grasp.

CHAPTER 2

More on Serial Transmission

In the preceding chapter we outlined some of the prerequisites for systems of data transfer. We will now consider one of the options, serial transfer of data, more closely.

It will be seen that there are two fundamentally different ways in which to go about transmitting data - asynchronously or synchronously. The difference centres around the ideal of whether or not it is wished to control the transfer exactly in time, with both transmitting and receiving devices being *synchronized*, i.e. bit transfer taking place at a preselected time and rate, or whether the exact timing, or rather sequence, of these events is to be somewhat arbitrary and even random.

Let us first consider the case of asynchronous transmission.

2.1 Asynchronous Transmission

From our description in the previous chapter, we have set up a simple system whereby we have one line, or wire, to carry the transmitted data. This will, by definition, when left alone be in a *rest state*. Let us then specify this state to be logic *high*, or positive.

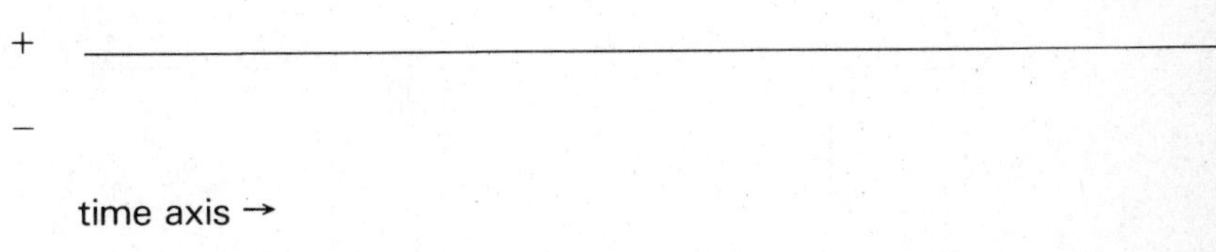

Fig. 2.1

This will be the input to the receiving device, and will be independent of time − the receiver will not mind how long the line stays at this high level. How then are we to indicate to the receiver that we are to commence transmission? The only way we have is to "pull" the line low, to minus or logic zero.

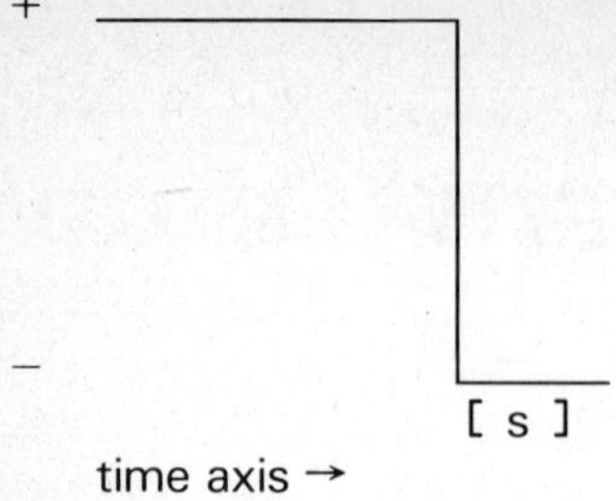

Fig. 2.2

It would be unwise to signify any real information in this simple switch of polarity. Remember, the receiving computer has been waiting for something to talk to it for who knows how long, and in being woken up will probably take a little time to pull itself together. This is, actually, found to be the case.

However, from now on the receiving device knows what to expect. Having been woken up by this first bit, or *start bit*, it will be expecting another eight bits of data (to make up the byte, which holds the code for our transmitted character). In fact, asynchronous transfer is really partially asynchronous, and partially synchronous. There may be long gaps, of any length, between individual characters, but when we have actually started transmitting a character, the system pulls itself together, and synchronizes. This is, of course, dependent on the transmitting and receiving devices knowing the length of time that individual bits will be present on the line, but it will be shown that this can be the case.

Thus as described before, we now place successive bits of data, starting for instance with the least significant bit, and ending up with the most significant bit, onto the transmit line.

Fig. 2.3

In the example of Fig. 2.3, we have the length (s) as the start bit, length (a) as the least significant bit (lsb), (b) as the next least significant bit, and so forth.

Thus our byte of data is, so far,

xxxxx110

where the x's are as yet untransmitted bits.

We continue this process, until the eight bits of the byte have been placed on the line.

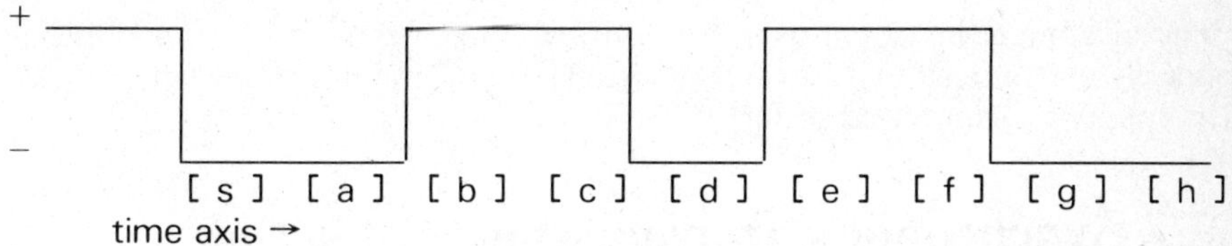

Fig. 2.4

We thus have, in this example,

a=0, b=1, c=1, d=0, e=1, f=1, g=0, h=0 ,

i.e. the byte is

00110110, or, in hexadecimal,

36H .

Looking in Appendix I, the ASCII Code conversion table, we see that this is in fact the number 6!

We now, of course, have to signify that this really is the end of the data. This is in fact only a formality – the receiving device will not be expecting any more bits to be sent, as it should have been expecting the full eight. However, there are cases, for instance if the two devices have not been set up correctly, where the addition of some end signal, naturally called the *stop bit*, can help. What is this stop bit to be? Logically, it should be the opposite of a start bit, and thus must be a logic one, or positive.

This, it will be seen, is actually the same as our rest state for the line, which will be seen to fit well into our scheme.

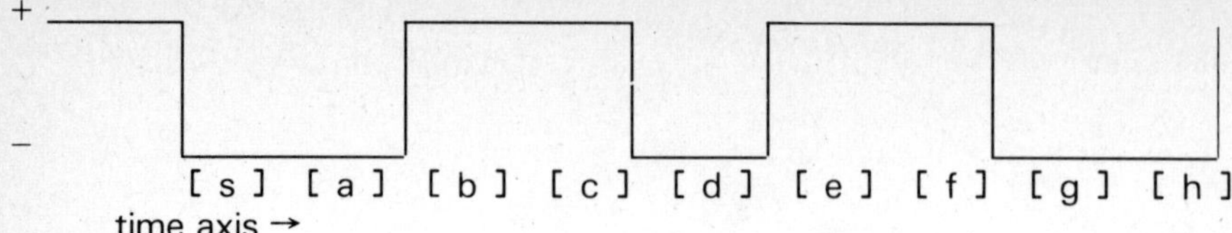

Fig. 2.5

The system now returns to its asynchronous state. The line is high, or positive, for an indeterminate amount of time, until another drop in the line is noticed – a new start bit.

The advantage, then, of an asynchronous system would seem to be that only one line is still required (apart from our "signal ground" mentioned earlier). So a lot of copper is being saved so far!

2.2 Synchronous Transmission – bit serial

Let us now instead consider how to synchronize all these events that are going on. It would appear from what has been discussed before that one line only is probably not enough – although we could have a continuous stream of bits being transmitted down the line, it would appear unlikely that this could be kept up ad infinitum without any error. Even computers slow down occasionally!

The most popular solution is the addition of a second line, called a *clock line*. As might be imagined from its name, this line is used to provide a regular series of pulses, like the ticking of a clock, to synchronize events. A system can now be devised to pair up corresponding bits with a clock pulse; if the receiving computer is keeping time with the clock signals, it can keep time with the bits that it is receiving.

Let us consider how such a system could be set up to work in practice.

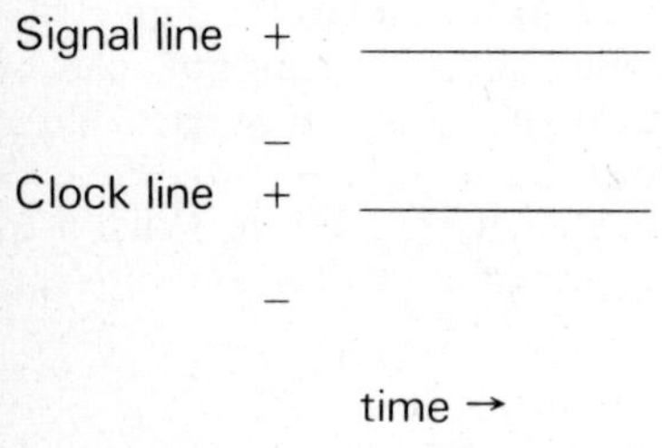

Fig. 2.6

The receiving device now watches the clock line. At present, both the clock line and signal line are held *high*, in their rest state. The first indication that something is going on is when a change is noted in the clock line – that is, when it changes from high to low.

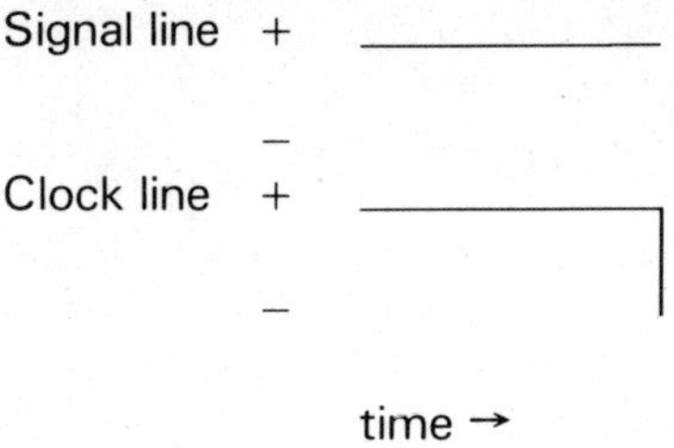

Fig. 2.7

The receiving device now knows that there is something going on – there will be some data on the signal line. It will be seen that there is already an advantage in this system – no start bit is required. The signal line may now be either high or low, that is, there may be no change in the state of line at all. All that the receiving machine has to do is to go and sample the signal line straight away, and record the value. There are thus two possibilities: either the signal line stays high (Fig. 2.8), or the signal line drops low (Fig. 2.9).

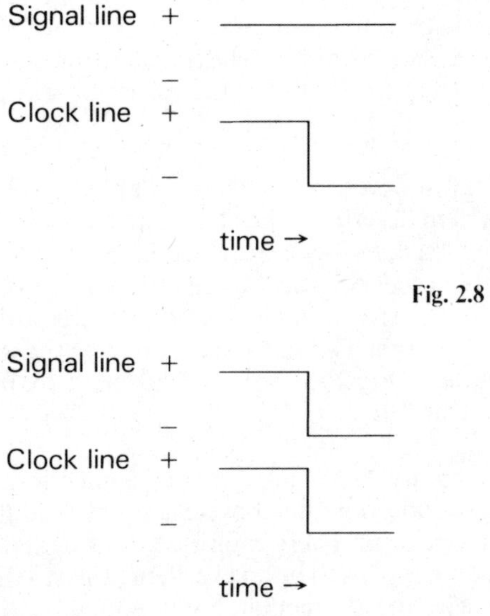

Fig. 2.8

Fig. 2.9

The clock line now returns to its original rest position, as does the signal line, indicating the end of transfer of one bit of data. This process can now continue for subsequent bits, until the whole byte, or indeed string of bytes, has been transfered.

e.g.

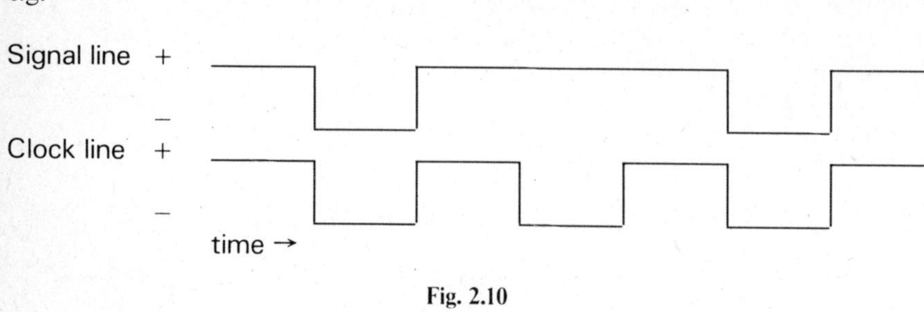

Fig. 2.10

In Fig. 2.10, the three bits 0, 1, and 0 have so far been transfered.

Of course, care must be taken that the pulsing on the clock line is not too fast for the receiving device to keep up with; a variation on the above theme (and there are many) could thus be that it is the *receiving device* that provides the clock pulse. This has the important advantage that the receiving device can now control exactly the rate of bit transfer. This system would work in a similar manner to the one previously described above, except that now the *transmitting device* will interrogate the clock line, waiting in a change in its state. When this change is noted, the next bit of data will be transmitted. The transmitting device will now wait for the clock line to return to its original state, whereupon it will likewise return the signal line to rest.

A further important improvement can, however, be made to the above system. It will be noted that, in the present system described, the clock line has to make a transition from high to low, and then back to high again, for each bit of data to be transmitted. This need not be the case. All that is actually required is to note a *change of state* in the clock line to signify a clock pulse, that is just a change from high to low, or from low to high. This effectively doubles the rate of transfer of bits. Thus in our example, in Fig.2.10, we now find that SIX bits have been transmitted, i.e. 0, 1, 1, 1, 0, and 1.

A clock line, then, is certainly a very handy device in data communication. It may pulse at a relatively slow pace, and indeed in the above examples need not even be regular, but conversely it may pulse at a very high rate, thus enabling rapid transfer of data. Now, a computer happens to be an excellent place to find a clock pulse – microprocessors themselves need a regular, high frequency clock provided to one of their inputs for basic operation. The slowest microprocessor chips tend to run at a frequency of at least 1 MHz (that's one million cycles per second!); nowadays clock frequencies tend to run at speeds of at least 4 MHz, or even up to 8 or 10 MHz. Thus there is, if required, a source of regular, clocked cycles to be called on. Of course one would not use such exceptionally high clock frequencies as 8 or 10 MHz (yet) for data transfer – a basic microprocessor instruction inside a chip itself takes many clock cycles of time to be executed. However, the clock frequency can be *divided down* to a more reasonable rate, a rate at which the microprocessor can be expected to keep up with as far as the data transfer mechanism goes, to provide a high frequency *clocked, bit synchronous* form of communication between computer devices.

2.3 A comparison of synchronous and asynchronous communication.

Why then, one might ask, is it that a relatively slow, inefficient system such as asynchronous communications is more popular? As most people are probably aware, if only from exposure to advertisements for printers, microcomputers and the like, everything nowadays seems to have an RS-232 interface on it. The RS-232 Interface Lead has even been satirised in popular television programmes!

Of course, one immediate disadvantage of using a clock line is that, (by definition!) an extra line has to be used. This may not be troublesome over short distances, say a few feet from one device in the same office as another, but it may prove troublesome over long distances. Another is to do with the electrical characteristics of data transmission over wires – at the end of the day, to make the system work, electrical currents have to be flying up and down the lines. Any universally useful system will have to be rugged, cheap on materials, and capable of working over reasonable distances. An acceptable compromise, it has been found, is to put up with an overall slower rate of data transfer.

2.4 Synchronous bit-parallel systems.

In section 2.2 the type of system described was for bit-serial transmission – the bits were transfered, in conjunction with a clock pulse, one after the other on the same physical line. This, it will be realized from the preceding discussions on serial and parallel transfer, need not necessarily have to be the case. Indeed, bit-parallel systems lend themselves admirably to having a clock line to keep the whole affair in order.

Consider the case of byte-parallel transfer, i.e. eight bits, and thus eight lines of data, at the same time. An extra clock line is now required (and a signal ground, as always), making nine significant lines in all.

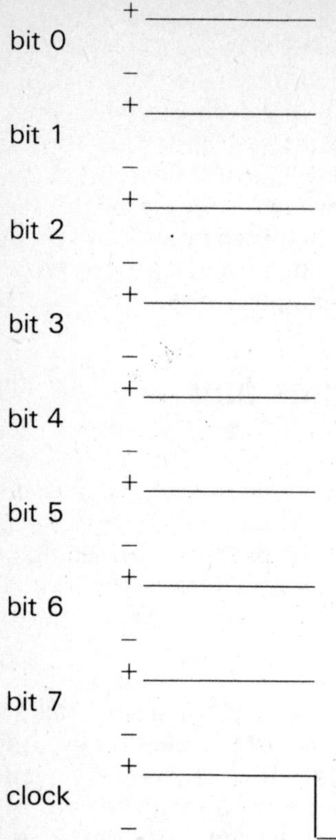

Thus with one pulse of the clock line, *eight* bits of data can be transferred in one go! This system is, indeed, most popular especially in applications of connecting a microcomputer up to a printer, and over short distances. But more on this in a later chapter.

CHAPTER 3

The RS-232 Serial Interface

We now come to a consideration of the RS-232 interface – perhaps the most important interface standard to consider, since it is by far, at the present time, the most widely used standard for communications in the computer industry.

In fact, its full title should be the EIA RS-232-C; EIA stands for the Electronic Industries Association, an American governing body based in Washington, and RS stands for Recommended Standard. Recommended Standard 232 (revision C) is just one of many specifications laid down by the EIA. There are others such as RS-423 (which is very similar to RS-232), and RS-422, which is of a fundamentally different nature. These will be considered in a later chapter.

There are two documents to support the RS-232-C standard. Both are available from the EIA. The standard itself is defined in one of these documents, called "Interface Between Data Terminal Equipment and Data Communication Equipment Employing Serial Data Interchange." The other is Industrial Electronics Bulletin Number 9, entitled "Application Notes for EIA Standard RS-232-C".

We have, in previous chapters, set out some of the parameters which need to be considered in configuring our communications system. In particular, the rate at which data, in the form of bits, can be transferred, the type of signal lines that are required, and the sort of distance over which our data can be successfully transfered.

According to the RS-232-C standard, electrical considerations determine that the maximum rate of data transfer is 20,000 bits per second, and only over relatively short lengths of cable, typically 50 feet or so. Despite some serious shortcomings, most of which have arisen by manufacturers not adhering strictly to the standards laid down by the EIA, the RS-232 remains exceptionally popular.

It will be noted in the title of the document which lays down the standard itself, reference is made to Data Terminal Equipment (DTE), and Data Communications Equipment (DCE). These terms, or at least their abbreviations, may have been encountered already – perhaps on the back of a microcomputer or modem, near the RS-232 socket. What do they mean?

3.1 DCE/DTE

It may be remembered that our simple system of bit-serial, asynchronous communication described so far has consisted of only one significant line – the transmission line. Of course, we also require the signal ground line as a voltage reference point, but it will transpire that there may be several other lines that are required as well.

In particular, we have so far considered only *one way* communication; that is, a transmitting and a receiving device. In practice we will normally be considering a situation in which we have two devices, each of which will be both transmitting and receiving – maybe at the same time!

It immediately becomes necessary to include one extra line, in order that we have one for signals going one way, and one for signals going the other way. You will start to feel a need, no doubt, for some standards to be laid down – which line is to be used for which direction? This is how the idea of DTE and DCE equipment comes about. Although (as with most things) there are strict historical reasons for its evolution, it is nowadays best, in order to avoid too much confusion, to merely consider the distinction between DTE and DCE as an arbitrary one. We have two devices, communicating with each other, say one on the left and one on the right.

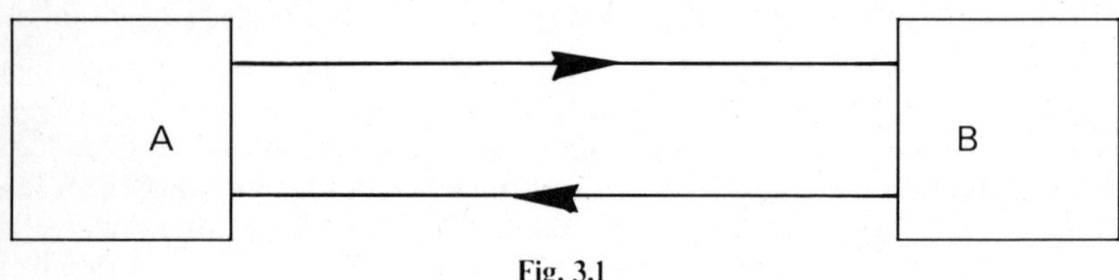

Fig. 3.1

We also have two lines; one must be used for A to send to B, and the other for B to send to A. It would be nice, then, to be able to specify, without fear of contradiction, exactly which device uses which line under any circumstance. We do not want them both to try transmitting on the same line!

Let us then define quite arbitrarily A as DTE, and B as DCE. Thus we always have the situation that DTE connects directly to DCE. If two DCE, or two DTE, devices are connected together, nothing will happen. (They will be both transmitting, and both receiving, on the same lines.)

In practice, however, since the RS-232 standard is generally used to connect a computer to a peripheral, such as a printer, a computer is designated as DTE, and the peripheral as DCE. As will be seen, it is not impossible to connect two computers together successfully, but one will have to be made to look like DCE. This is not as drastic as it may sound – all that is required is a wiring change – but it is the root of many people's confusion.

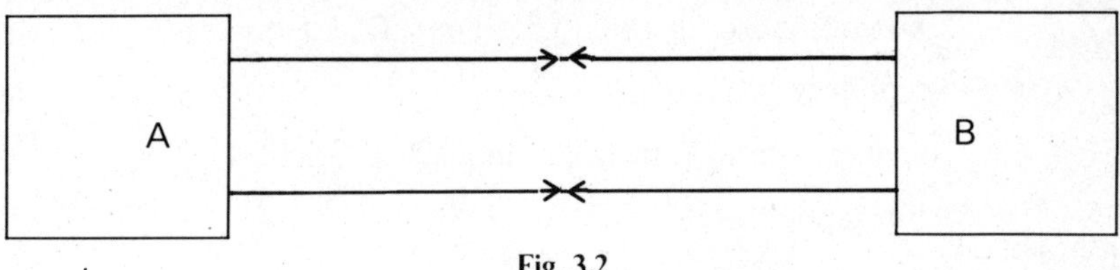

Fig. 3.2

We have thus defined our two distinctive types of equipment, but have not yet exactly defined which wires are going to be used in practice for transmitting and receiving. Let us then consider in detail the actual *hardware* that is required – plugs, sockets and wires.

3.2 Signal Lines

We have so far specified the need for three lines – one for DTE to transmit to DCE, one for DCE to transmit to DTE, and a ground. In actual fact, RS-232 provides for 22 lines! Moreover, the specification for plugs and sockets is that they should have 25 pin connections – see the section on mechanical specifications.

Pin Number	Description
1	Protective ground
2	Transmitted data (TxD)
3	Received data (RxD)
4	Request to Send (RTS)
5	Clear to Send (CTS)
6	Data Set Read (DSR)
7	Signal Ground (Common Return)
8	Data Carrier Detect (DCD or CD)
9	(Reserved for data set testing)
10	(Reserved for data set testing)
11	(Unassigned)

12	Secondary DCD
13	Secondary CTS
14	Secondary TxD
15	Transmitter Signal Timing Element (DCE Source)
16	Secondary RxD
17	Receiver Signal Timing Element (DCE Source)
18	(Unassigned)
19	Secondary RTS
20	Data Terminal Ready (DTR)
21	Signal Quality Detector
22	Ring Indicator
23	Data Signal Rate Selector (DTE/DCE Source)
24	Transmitter Signal Element Timing (DTE Source)
25	(Unassigned)

There are, in fact, far more lines catered for than are usually ever needed. As will be seen from a cursory inspection of the above table, two independent transmit/receive systems are catered for. Normally only the primary circuits are used.

It will be noted that there is provision for one receive line and one transmit line. What does this mean? Our original ideas pointed us towards needing one line for DTE to transmit to DCE, and one line for DCE to transmit to DTE. The RS-232 specification, however, takes the viewpoint of only one of these devices – *the data terminal equipment*. This is unfortunately a source of confusion. DTE transmits to DCE using pin 2 – the TxD line. DCE, on the other hand, *transmits* to DTE using pin 3, the so-called *receive* line RxD . So from the viewpoint of *data communications equipment*, pin 2 is actually the receive line, and pin 3 is actually the transmit line.

There are actually not many other important lines to consider. The ones in general daily use are:

RTS, CTS, DSR, DTR, and DCD.

Before each of the lines is considered individually in detail, a word must be said about the actual line levels, that is voltage levels, employed in the RS-232 standard.

It will be seen from the above descriptions that there are four distinct types of signal lines used:

a)   data signals, such as transmitted or received data
b)   control signals, such as RTS, CTS
c)   timing signals (like the clock lines discussed already)
d)   signal grounds

Control signals and timing signals are considered to be ON when *positive*, and OFF when *negative*.

Unfortunately, data signals are not quite so straightforward. The signals are effectively inverted. That is, they arc considered to be a mark (logic 1) when negative, and a space (logic 0) when positive.

Let us now consider the lines in detail.

Pin 1, Protective Ground.
This connects to the metal frame of the equipment, both DCE and DTE. It usually also shields the interconnecting cable, and thus ensures that the frames of both machines are at the same ground potential.

Pin 2, Transmitted Data (TXD).
This is data transmitted from DTE to DCE. DTE should hold the signal line in a mark state (that is, logic 1 or high), both when there is nothing being transmitted, and also in between characters and words, i.e. bits and bytes. Also, the specification for RS-232 stipulates that DTE should not transmit any data unless all four of the following signal lines are ON, (i.e. *positive*): RTS, CTS, DSR & DTR.

Pin 3, Received Data (RXD).
This is data transmitted from DCE to DTE, i.e. data received by DTE from DCE. This signal line is held in a mark state (logic 1), when the DCD signal line is in an OFF condition (negative). In a *half-duplex* system (which will be explained later), furthermore, the signal line must be in a mark state (logic 1) when RTS is *on*, i.e. positive

Pin 4, Request To Send (RTS).
This signal is generated *by DTE only*. Basically, when RTS is in an ON condition, it tells DCE to start to transmit. When in an OFF condition, conversely, it tells DCE to stop transmitting. When the signal line is pulled from off to on, the DCE should respond by turning ON the CTS signal line. DTE should transmit data to DCE only when CTS is on. Finally, if RTS is turned off, it must not be turned on again until DCE has replied by turning off CTS.

Pin 5, Clear To Send (CTS).

This signal is, conversely, generated *by DCE only*. When this signal line is held on, it indicates to DTE that the DCE is ready to transmit. But a more important use for CTS is that, as specified above, DTE should not transmit to DCE unless CTS is ON.

Pin 6, Data Set Ready (DSR).

This signal, in a similar manner to CTS, is generated *by DCE only*. It deals with the status of the local data set. Strictly, it is turned on by DCE to indicate that it has attempted to establish a communications channel, and has completed any start-up tasks that may be necessary. In practice, it is used to indicate to DTE that everything is ready to go.

Pin 7, Signal Ground, or Common Return.

This line is used to provide a reference potential for all other lines in the RS-232, except of course for the Protective Ground (pin 1). Of course, it could be at any potential in relation to protective ground; in practice it is usually set to be at 0V, whilst ON may be between +3V and +12V, and OFF may be between -3V and -12V.

Pin 8, Data Carrier Detect (DCD).

DCD is generated by DCE. Again, strictly speaking, DCE should put this signal line ON when it is receiving a signal "which meets its suitability criteria". In reality its uses vary, but it is often used by DCE on DTE to disable data reception.

Pins 9 to 11 are used for test purposes, or unspecified.

Pin 12, Secondary Received Line Signal Detector. (Secondary DCD).

This signal line functions in the same way as for DCD (pin 8, above), but refers to the secondary channels for DCE/DTE.

Pin 13, Secondary Clear To Send.

As for CTS.

Pin 14, Secondary Transmitted Data.

As for pin 2, Transmitted Data, but it is used to transmit via a secondary channel, which is usually of a lower speed.

Pin 15, Transmitter Signal Timing Element. (DCE Source)

This signal line is controlled by DCE. It is used to provide signal timing for DTE. Thus DTE will send data on its transmit line only, strictly, on an OFF to ON transition of this line.

Pin 16, Secondary Received Data.
As for Received Data, pin 3, but in a similar manner to pin 14, Secondary Transmitted Data, it is used for a secondary channel.

Pin 17, Receiver Signal Element Timing (DCE Source)
This is a particular kind of clock timing signal, provided by DCE. It is used to indicate to DTE when the signal on the Received Data signal line is at the centre of a bit. (This is the line that is used by DCE to transmit to DTE). Strictly, an ON to OFF transition indicates the centre of each bit.

Pin 18, Unassigned.

Pin 19, Secondary Request To Send.
As for RTS (signal line 4), but for the secondary channel.

Pin 20, Data Terminal Ready. (DTR)
This is the last of the important lines in the RS-232, and is widely used. This signal line is controlled *by DTE only*. Its use in general is to indicate, when ON, to DCE that everything is ready. Strictly, when ON it indicates to DCE that it is all right to maintain an established communication channel (between DCE and a remote DCE); if in an OFF condition, DCE should abort the communication channel upon the completion of any data transfer in progress.

Pin 21, Signal Quality Detector.
This signal line is controlled by DCE, and should normally be ON. If set to OFF, it is an indication by DCE that there is a high probability of error in the transmitted signal.

Pin 22, Ring Indicator.
This signal, too, is controlled by DCE, and is used for instance when DCE is hooked up to a modem. If ON, it indicates to DTE that a ringing signal is being received by DCE. It is otherwise in an OFF condition.

Pin 23, Data Signal Rate Selector (DCE/DTE Source).
The source for this signal line may be either DCE or DTE, but not both at the same time. If it is DTE that is controlling it, an ON state indicates to DCE that when a dual transfer rate system is being used, then the higher of the two rates should be employed. Conversely, if OFF, the lower rate should be used. The rate can be determined similarly by DCE.

Pin 24, Transmitter Signal Element timing (DTE source).
This is the last of the signal lines used in RS-232, and operates in a similar manner to its counterpart, the Transmit Signal Element Timing (DCE source), pin 15.

Pin 25, Unassigned.

3.3 Electrical Specifications

The EIA RS-232-C specification, as well as laying down the specification for signal lines used, also specifies the electrical requirements of the circuitry to be used. For instance, as stated before, an ON condition is indicated by a positive voltage, and an OFF condition by a negative voltage. But what level of voltage should be used? RS-232 specifies that a positive voltage must be greater than $+3V$, and a negative voltage less than $-3V$.

Moreover, the circuitry used for receiving should be able to withstand a voltage of up to $+25V$, and down to $-25V$. So in practice, our positive voltage should be in the range $+3V$ to $+25V$, and our negative voltage similarly between $-3V$ and $-25V$. This suits today's TTL logic circuit design well; nominal voltages here are of the order of $+$ or $-5V$.

Also, the circuitry used to drive the transmitting lines should be able to withstand a short across its lines, that is it should not break down if the transmit line is connected to circuit or protective ground. It should also be able to withstand a short between any of the signal lines, as might happen in a broken or damaged cable for instance. Furthermore, if a short were to occur, then the resulting current should not be greater than 500mA.

It will be noted that there is a range of voltage levels, from $-3V$ to $+3V$, that is not defined as specifying either ON or OFF. Signal ground lies in this region, by definition, at 0V. This region is known as the *transition region*.

As regards the control signal lines, such as the RTS and CTS lines, the standard specifies that when a switch is made on these lines from ON to OFF, or from OFF to ON, then the time spent in the transition region should be less than 1 millisecond. For data and timing signals, such as data on the transmit or receive lines, the time in this transition region should be no more than 1ms, or 4% of the signal element duration time (whichever is less).

3.4 Plugs & Sockets.

Confusion abounds, unfortunately, over the subject of plugs and sockets, male and female. This is not helped by manufacturers choosing to use plugs or sockets almost at random. The RS-232 standard does not specify any particular type of connector, apart from the specification of having 25 pins, but it does make some recommendations. Fortunately, manufacturers have standardized on the type of connector used – a 25 pin D-type, such as is produced by Amphenol and Cannon. Although the standard for RS-232 does specify that DCE should be female, this is certainly not adhered to, probably because some people do not agree on what is male and what is female!

A plug (male), fits into a socket (female). Unfortunately with the 25 pin D-type connector, both of the types could be, under different definitions, be described as either plug or socket. We will follow what are hopefully by now the most widespread of conventions:

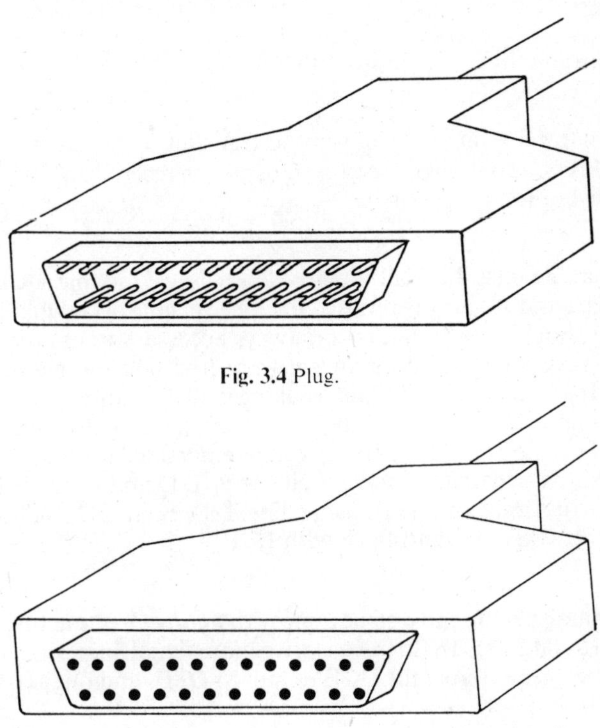

Fig. 3.4 Plug.

Fig. 3.5 Socket.

Thus, our "plug" is seen to be by some as a socket, in that although it consists of 25 pins which stick out, and thus insert into a socket, it also has an outer protective cover which encloses all of the pins internally; it thus becomes a socket, into which something is plugged!

3.5 RS-232 In The Real World.

The preceding description of the specifications laid down for the RS-232 standard has been for reference, and hopefully some amusement, only. As with most things in life, the reality is rather different.

Whilst many of the available pins may be used, it is very rare for more than seven or eight to be used. Indeed, most systems will be able to cope with just two or three.

In a loose order of necessity, to give a rough idea of how important the line is or how often it is used, the most common signal lines are as follows:

1) Signal ground   (always there)

2) Transmit/receive lines: if you want to transmit or receive anything (which is what all this is about!) you need a transmit or receive line. This may be TxD or RxD, or both.

3) Handshaking lines: basically, handshaking is used so that DCE may tell DTE when to start and stop transmitting, and vice versa. This is what the *control line* signals are about. However, it is not always necessary to use the signal lines, as the handshaking can be done in *software* (the controlling communications program). If this is the case, the handshaking is all done using our existing transmit and receive lines. For handshaking *control characters* (the ones that are in the ASCII table at the back of the book), can be embedded in the string of data being transmitted. Notice that we now require *both* TxD and RxD - if DTE transmits to DCE for instance on the transmit line TxD, then DCE will have to use its transmit line, RxD, to handshake with DTE.

However, handshaking can also be done with *hardware* (the actual physical signal lines), such as RTS or CTS. In this case two more signal lines, which will be control lines, will be needed – one for DCE to talk to DTE, and one for DTE to talk to DCE.

4) DSR and DTR handshakes: the next most usual lines to be found being used are another set of hardware handshaking lines – DSR and DTR. Their use is usually superfluous.

5) A final hardware handshaking line is sometimes included – DCD (as if there were not enough already!).

6) Unassigned lines: it is rare to see, or to need to use, any other signal lines. However, some manufacturers such as Epson use a rather non-standard configuration for their printers, in that pin 11, which you will remember is unassigned, for a hardware handshake line, instead of RTS (pin 4).

In summary, the most likely arrangements to see are:

	2, 3, and 7
or,	2, 3, 4, 5, and 7
or,	2, 3, 4, 5, 6, and 20
or,	2, 3, 4, 5, 6, 8, and 20.

In the following chapter we shall consider the real mechanics of how to transmit data from one device to another — you will remember our initial ideas of start bits, stop bits and the eight bits to make up a byte of data. Lets see how it all works in practice.

CHAPTER 4

Asynchronous Data Transmission

We will now concentrate for a time on the practicalities and realities of asynchronous serial data transmission, via the RS-232. We know we have a nice system set up ready to use - a transmit and a receive line, a signal ground for reference, and plenty of hardware handshaking lines, should we need them! We also have some idea of the voltages, currents and timings available to us, and have outlined already our proposal for transmitting successive bits of data from one device to another. What have we, so far, not considered?

4.1 Start Bit

As discussed in a previous chapter, we need some way of indicating to the receiving device that data is on its way. The way that is used in RS-232 is by using a *start bit*. This is simply a transition of our transmit line from its rest state (which is high, or logic zero), to the opposite – low, or logic one. Thus a start bit is simply a bit of value 1.

4.2 Baud Rates

Our next problem is to decide the speed at which we send data "down the line". What we need to be concerned with is the length of time that a bit of data is present on the signal line, and hence the number of bits that can be transmitted over a given period of time.

Suppose we have one device talking to another, and that the DTE is transmitting to the DCE. Then, it will be using pin 2 of our connectors – that is TXD.

Our data bit to be transmitted will either be a "1" or a "0", i.e. we will be representing it as either a negative or a positive voltage. (Remember that, unfortunately, in RS-232 parlance our signals our inverted – 0 is represented by a positive voltage, and 1 by a negative voltage). Suppose, then, that we wish to send a "1" bit.

Now, in a rest state, our transmit line will be "high", or positive (i.e. logic 0), as in Fig. 4.1.

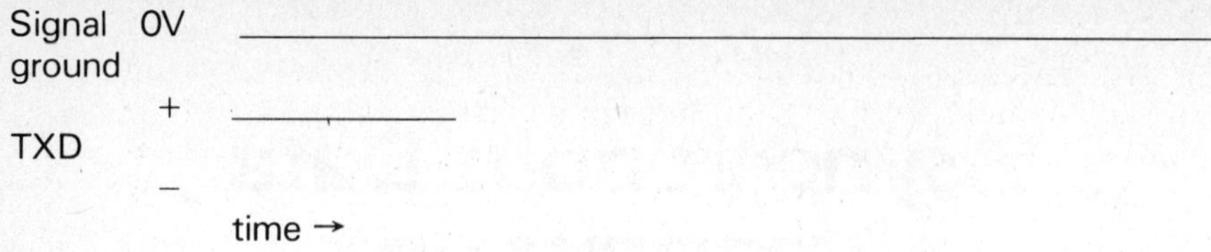

Fig. 4.1

To signify a one bit on the transmit line, we set its value to negative. This value will have to be maintained for some time to give the DCE, which is receiving the signal, a chance to register the change. Thus, after this time, we can set the voltage level corresponding to our next bit value. If this is to be another "1", then the line signal can remain where it is, i.e. in a negative state. However, if our next bit of data is a "0", we will have to "pull" the line high, to a positive state.

This process will continue for our eight bits of the byte of data to be transfered.

In order to know what length of time to hold our value on the line, all we need to tell both devices is *number of bits per second* that we are going to transmit. This is usually called the *baud rate*. (Strictly, baud rate and bits per second are not exactly the same thing, although close enough for usual purposes).

All computer manufacturers agree on a number of standard values of baud rates to be used. Remember, too, that RS-232 is not guaranteed according to the standard laid down to perform above 20,000 bits per second. Common baud rates are as follows:

50, 75, 110, 150, 300, 600, 1200, 2400, 4800, 9600, 19200.

Different types of situations sometimes require different baud rates. Perhaps the most usual baud rate to come across is 9600. This is generally used for connecting terminals to computers, connecting microcomputers to printers, and connecting one computer to another. However, when connecting a computer to a modem, or acoustic coupler, (more on these later – they are devices to translate our RS-232 signals into other signals that can be transmitted over telephone lines) one of three possibilities is generally used – .

300/300 that is, transmit and receive baud rates are both set to 300

1200/1200 similarly, the baud rates are set to 1200

or

1200/75 or 75/1200. Our transmit and receive baud rates need not be the same, although they are normally.

Of course it is usually best to use the highest baud rate possible – it means that your data can be transferred faster, thus tying up the resources of your machinery for a shorter time. Unfortunately a baud rate of 19200 is not usually found to be very successful – most machines cannot keep up with it, and indeed many machines do not even cater for it. There are, on the other hand, sometimes advantages in slowing the data transfer rate down. For instance, it is probably fairly obvious when using a telephone for normal conversation that the quality is not usually very good. In order to minimize the risk of data being corrupted, it is found to be best to transfer the data at a slower rate – say 300 baud as above – although this may mean it taking longer to transmit a whole file, for instance. But better safe than sorry!

Consider, also, the case of a central computer (perhaps a mainframe or a supermini) with a number of terminals connected to it. The computer may have to cope with servicing one, two, ten or perhaps twenty terminals all at the same time. Each terminal may have an operator on it, frantically typing away at the computer. If the computer is unable to cope with servicing all the terminals at a high baud rate of, say, 9600, it may be best to drop the speed to a more suitable level.

4.3 Parity

You will probably have realized by now that there is going to be a lot of data flying up and down our signal lines. How are we to know whether or not the data becomes corrupted along the way? We might "drop" a bit!

Fortunately RS-232 is generally very reliable; certainly, when connecting one device to another over a short distance by means of a physical cable. However, there are cases, especially when transmitting over telephone lines (where "noise" on the line can cause "glitches", or unwanted spikes, to appear) when things are not so reliable. In these cases it is possible to devise a system for error checking, although not, in this system, error correcting.

Consider what has been transmitted so far : one start bit, and seven or eight data bits. (Remember out byte of data is eight bits, although for ASCII code we require only seven bits to be sent – however we may be sending EBCDIC code which requires the full eight bits). What we can do is to transmit *one extra bit*, called the *parity bit*. As its name implies, it conveys in some sense the parity of the string of bits transmitted. For supposing we sent a string of bits thus:

1 00111011

i.e. a start bit and eight data bits.

Then we have sent a start bit, then 5 1's, and 3 0's. Let us add the parity bit, say another "0" :

    1 00111011 0

By definition this is of odd parity, since we have an odd number of "1" 's in our stream of data after the start bit, including the parity bit. Conversely, we could have sent an extra 1:

    1 00111011 1

which would have been parity even.

So, if your byte of data has an odd number of bits, and if you require parity odd, then the parity bit is zero. However, if there is an even number of bits the parity bit is one, to maintain odd parity. The converse is true for even parity.

Thus if our transmitting machine is set, say, to parity even, it will transmit the stream in our second example above. Of course our receiving device must also be configured the same – to parity even. Now the receiving device accepts the transmitted bits one by one, and stores them away. After receiving the eight data bits it will know to expect a further bit, the parity bit. But suppose ther has been an error on our transmit line, and what the device has actually received (including the start bit) is:

    1 00101011

One of our bits has changed from 1 to 0. The receiving device will know that it has received four ones – furthermore, it will be expecting (if it has done its calculations correctly) a parity bit of 0. However, it receives a parity bit of 1, and thus knows that something has gone wrong with the data transmission. If it is a smart communications program, it might put up a message on the VDU of "PARITY ERROR", or something similar.

There are a number of standard choices for parity:

NONE, ODD, EVEN, MARK, and SPACE. (Not all of these are always available, although there should always be the choice of at least the first three).

ODD and EVEN are explained above, but what of the others?

MARK and SPACE are straight forward. MARK, you will remember, is our logic 1 state (that means, with our confusing inversion, a negative voltage); *parity mark* simply means that the parity bit is set always to 1. Conversely, *parity space* means that the parity bit is set always to 0.

Parity none should be straightforward – no parity bit is set. However, slight confusion is caused sometimes by one interpretation that it means the same as parity space – i.e. parity set to zero, but this is not its usual interpretation.

Unfortunately, the idea of setting a single parity bit to check for errors in transmission is not infallible. From our original example above, it will be seen that if the case were to arise that *two* "1" bits were to be dropped, then the parity of the string of transmitted "1"'s would be restored, and our receiving device would not be aware of any error in the transmitted byte. Hopefully, however, the probability of dropping just a single bit will be so low that the probability of dropping two bits in the same byte will not worry us too much!

There are other, more sophisticated, methods of avoiding errors in data transfer, which will be discussed in a later chapter.

4.4 Data Bits and Stop Bits

You will remember that we are sticking to using our ASCII code to translate our everyday letters and numbers into a byte of data. However, you will also recall that ASCII requires only 7 bits, whilst EBCDIC requires all the 8 bits in a byte. This brings us to another parameter that can usually be set up when configuring a communications package – the number of data bits to be sent. The choice is usually between 7 and 8, although you may sometimes see the possibility of having just 5 or 6 bits sent per character of data.

It will normally be wasteful to have to send 8 bits for every ASCII character transmitted – we would be wasting time sending an extra bit for every character. However, suppose we had a system, say a Telex type service, which required only capital letters and numbers to be sent. Then with a bit of thought, and a good deal of staring at the ASCII character table, you could see that we only need 6 bits per character (by suitably rearranging or "compressing" the data). This would mean that we save having to send another bit for every character, which may prove to be most advantageous if our system has to transmit at a slow speed, for instance.

Finally, you will remember our idea of finishing off the transmission of each stream of bits for a character with a stop bit. This is really just equivalent to returning the transmit signal line to its normal state, and ensuring that it stays in this state for a certain amount of time (the standard amount of time that we are giving each bit in transmission). In fact, there is normally a choice of the number of stop bits that we are going to send – either one or two. This is a slightly arbitrary distinction, since one stop bit and a wait before sending another character is indistinguishable from two stop bits. However, if there is to be no delay between sending successive characters down the line, then it may be the case that the receiving machine needs a little more time than usual to process the incoming data, and hence requires two stop bits. In practice, setting the option of having two stop bits is used only when using very slow baud rates, such as 300 or 150, or lower.

4.5 The Data Stream

You will have gathered by now that there must be lots of different combinations of ways to send our data. Do not worry—there is only one thing to remember. *It does not really matter, as long as both the transmitting and receiving devices are set up in the same way.*

Let us consider some combinations, and see what advantages or disadvantages they possess. We could have, for instance:

a) 1 start bit, 7 data bits, no parity, one stop bit.

This is the most compact way of sending 7-bit ASCII code. It has only two possible disadvantages—there is no parity bit, so we have no means of checking whether the data has been sent correctly. The second possible disadvantage is that it requires only nine bits in our data stream. Whilst this is in many ways a positive advantage, for it means we have less bits to send and thus makes for faster transfer of a whole file, it may also be a problem in that some of the hardware (i.e. the microprocessor chip etc.) that we are using may not be able to send as few as nine bits. For instance, there is a range of microprocessors produced by Hitachi (more of which in a later chapter) which have, included in them, SERIAL INPUT-OUTPUT (SIO). We have a choice of only two possible total-length data streams—a stream of 10 bits or a stream of 11 bits. Thus if we are constrained to using this type of microprocessor, we will not be able to send just 9 bits.

Let us then consider the possibilities of sending a 10 bit stream. We could have:

b) 1 start bit, 8 data bits, 1 stop bit or

c) 1 start bit, 7 data bits, 2 stop bits or

d) 1 start bit, 7 data bits, 1 parity bit, 1 stop bit.

Format (b) is fine for ASCII, and also EBCDIC, code, but contains no parity bit. Format (c) is much the same as format (a) above, but has two stop bits instead of one. This is usually superfluous, but may be necessary for slow-speed communication.

Format (c) is ideal for ASCII – we can now set a parity bit (normally to either odd or even; there is no advantage, although even is generally preferred) and contain the whole data stream in just 10 bits.

Some of the above formats may actually turn out to be the same. For instance, if we use (b) to send ASCII code, then since the least significant bit is sent first and the most significant bit is sent last, and since the most significant bit will always be zero (since ASCII requires only seven bits, remember), this is equivalent to

   1 start bit, 7 data bits, space parity, 1 stop bit.

Also, our format (c) is always equivalent to

   1 start bit, 7 data bits, mark parity, 1 stop bit

since the receiving device could equally decipher the parity bit (which will always be set to a "1") as a stop bit, which is also always a "1".

Moving on to a stream of 11 bits, we could have:

e) 1 start bit, 7 data bits, 1 parity bit, 2 stop bits or

f) 1 start bit, 8 data bits, 2 stop bits or

g) 1 start bit, 8 data bits, 1 parity bit, 1 stop bit.

Format (e) would not generally be useful, whilst format (g) would be ideal when it was necessary to send a full eight bits per character.

Finally, consider

h) 1 start bit, 8 data bits, 1 parity bit, 2 stop bits

which is a total length of 12 bits, but is not generally used; you may recall, there is usually a requirement for two stop bits only when using very slow baud rates.

4.6 Other Serial Interfaces

The RS-232 interface is by far the most widely used in the computer industry, despite its limitations and slight lack of real standardization, due to manufacturers adopting their own ideas about standards. However, the microcomputer industry is subject to change, as with the rest of the world; this change is often fast and furious, with new operating systems and diskette standards trying to keep up with advances in microprocessor technology. Communications, too, are not immune to change, but by the very nature of the industry (there are a lot of machines out there with RS-232 interfaces!), the change is perhaps not so fast. Whilst an upgrade to a new type of computer, which is bigger, better, and faster, is often not only desirable but also necessary to keep pace with new demands on processing power, it would not be very popular to have to change all the associated collection of add-ons every time, such as printers, plotters and modems. For this reason RS-232 is still supported wholeheartedly by manufacturers.

Nevertheless change must come, and in order to accommodate this the Electronic Industries Association released a new set of standards for communications. Fortunately these new standards do not differ radically from those originally laid down for RS-232 – indeed the aim has been to update the RS-232 standard, and provide compatibility between the old and the new during the transition period.

The two main problems with RS-232 have been found to be the limitation of interconnecting cable to about fifty feet (many offices nowadays would require greater distances between terminals and computers, for instance), and the limitation of transfer rates to less than 20,000 bits per second. In order to accommodate changes to these, the EIA released three new standards, which are RS-449, RS-422-A and RS-423-A.

You may have come across some or all of these already. For instance Acorn, the manufacturer of the BBC microcomputer, has from the start used an RS-423 interface on the back of the computer instead of the normal RS-232. Whilst this interface does not use the standard 25-pin D-type connector (it has a 5-pin DIN type socket instead), the signal levels are compatible with RS-232, and in effect the interface can be used just as if it were RS-232.

The first standard, RS-449, concerns itself only with the functional and mechanical characteristics of the standards, whilst RS-422-A and RS-423-A concern themselves with the electrical characteristics of the interface. As with the RS-232, the EIA released documents covering the new standards. For the RS-449 these are:

"General Purpose 37-Position and 9-Position Interface for Data Terminal Equipment and Data Circuit-Terminating Equipment Employing Serial Binary Data Interchange"

and

"Application Notes on Interconnection Between Interface Circuits Using RS-449 and RS-232-C".

For the RS-422-A the document is

"Electrical Characteristics of Balanced Voltage Digital Interface Circuits"

whilst for the RS-423-A the document is

"Electrical Characteristics of Unbalanced Voltage Digital Interface Circuits".

RS-449

Let us first consider the RS-449 standard. As one would expect with an upgrading of a standard as widespread and popular as RS-232, the basic functions remain the same for RS-449. However, there are some important differences. For instance, the maximum rate of data transfer is raised from 20k bits per second (that is, 20,000) to 2M bits per second (i.e. over 2 million). The connector standards are changed – gone is the faithful friend, the 25-pin D-type. Of less concern to us, but of great concern to electronic engineers and designers, is that there are changes to circuits and circuit functions. For instance, ten new circuit functions have been included, whilst three original RS-232 circuit functions have gone.

New circuit standards have to be introduced to cope with the introduction of this new, high speed, transfer specification. You would imagine that if RS-232 was restricted to 20K bits/s, and in fact tends to stick to less than half that speed, i.e. a baud rate of 9600, then there would be a very good reason for it. Indeed there is; however, we will not concern ourselves with an in-depth study of the associated electronics here.

However, the RS-449 specification does not have the freedom to specify any new standards it would like – remember that RS-232 is very well established in the computer world, and has to be catered for. Thus the RS-449 standard is, in computer jargon, "downward compatible" with RS-232 – it does RS-232 and more, and so can still be interfaced easily to RS-232.

In order to accommodate this downward compatibility, two different types of circuits need to be specified for the actual data transfer. You can probably well imagine that, since the old RS-232 type circuits could not work above 20K bits/s, (and certainly not at such a high rate as 2M bits/s), then the sort of circuit required for high rate transfer would not be compatible with our RS-232. It is for this reason, that the *unbalanced* circuits of the RS-232 are replaced, in the RS-422, with *balanced* circuits to accommodate the high speed transfer. However, the unbalanced type are still catered for in the RS-423 specification.

Now, RS-449 specifies two *categories* of circuits for driving the signal lines – CATEGORY I circuits and CATEGORY II circuits. CATEGORY I circuits are those which are capable of transferring signals at the high rate of 2M bits/s; conversely, CATEGORY II circuits use only unbalanced signals, and are thus suitable only for the slower rate of data transfer. There are ten extra circuits in RS-449 to accommodate these category I circuits; in fact, each of these may utilize either balanced (and hence high speed) or unbalanced (and hence low speed) circuit design, depending on the data transfer speed that is required in the design.

You will no doubt remember from the RS-232 specification that a secondary channel was incorporated. This was one of the reasons why it was necessary to have to use the rather cumbersome 25 pin D-type connector, which is particularly annoying when, as is most often the case, you require to use only three or perhaps five signal lines. Fortunately, in RS-449, the secondary channel is relegated to using a separate connector, which is this time a small, convenient 9 pin D-type. However, due to the addition of the ten circuits for our balanced line signals, our main connector unfortunately becomes a 37 pin D-type! Naturally, if the secondary channel is not required, then at least the 9 pin D-type connector can be omitted.

Let us work our way through the 37 signal lines, giving a brief description of their function and listing their category.

Pin 1.

As with the RS-232, this is a ground or shield line.

Pin 2. Category II. Signal Rate Indicator.

This signal line is controlled by DCE, and as with RS-232 is used to inform DTE which one of two data signaling rates DCE is using. When this line is ON, then the higher of the two rates is being used.

Pin 3. This line is spare.

Pin 4. Category I. Send Data.

This signal line, which is controlled by DTE, is just like TxD of the RS-232, and is used in exactly the same way.

Pin 5. Category I. Send Timing.

DCE controls this signal line. It is a clock line used to synchronize bit transfer from the DTE. The DTE should provide one bit of information on the send line each time this signal line goes from OFF to ON.

Pin 6. Category I. Receive Data.

This signal line is just like RxD of the RS-232. It is the receive data line, and is used for data transfer from the DCE to the DTE.

Pin 7. Category I. Request To Send.

This line functions like RTS (Request To Send). It is used by the DTE to control the transmit function of the DCE.

Pin 8. Category I. Receive Timing.

This line has a similar function to pin 5, Send Timing, described above. It is provided by the DCE, and a transition of its value from ON to OFF indicates the centre of each signal element, or bit of data, on the receive data line (pin 6).

Pin 9. Category I. Clear To Send.

In exactly the same way as the CTS signal line in RS-232, this line is controlled by the DCE, and is used to indicate to the DTE that the DCE is in a state of data transmission. If CTS is low, then DTE should not transmit to the DCE.

(In addition to having CTS ON, the following signal lines should also be ON: Request To Send, Data Mode, Terminal Ready and Terminal in Service).

Pin 10. Category II. Local Loopback.

This signal line is used by the DTE to indicate to the DCE that the DTE is requesting a test of the functionality of the DTE-DCE interface that has been set up.

Pin 11. Category I. Data Mode.

This signal line is used to indicate to the DTE the status of the attached DCE. Basically, the DCE can normally be used to communicate with the DTE if it is not tied up with any other function, if it is hooked up to the transfer channels necessary, and if it has completed any necessary call-up functions. In this case, the Data Mode is ON.

If this signal line is in the OFF condition, the the DTE should disregard any signals it receives from the DCE except for: Incoming Call, Test Mode or Standby Indicator.

Pin 12. Category I. Terminal Ready.

This line is controlled by the DTE, and is similar in functioning to the DTR (Data Terminal Ready) of the RS-232 interface.

Pin 13. Category I. Receiver Ready.

This, in a manner similar to pin 12, Terminal Ready, emulates the RS-232 line DSR (Data Set Ready). It is used by the DCE to indicate to the DTE that it is ready to receive data.

Pin 14. Category II. Remote Loopback.

This is another test line - if it goes ON, then it indicates to the local DCE that it should signal a remote loopback test with a *remote* DCE, by putting Test Mode (pin 18) ON.

Pin 15. Category II. Incoming Call.

This line is used, whn ON, to indicate that a ringing call is being received by the local DCE. It is OFF at all other times.

Pin 16. Category II. Select Frequency/Signaling Rate Selector.

These two functions share the same pin.

The Select Frequency signal originates from the DTE, and is used to control the transmit and receive frequency bands of the DCE as follows:

if Select Frequency is ON, then the higher band is allocated to transmit, and the lower band to receive;

if Select Frequency is OFF, then the higher band is now allocated to receive, and the lower band to transmit.

Pin 17. Category I. Terminal Timing.

This signal is provided by the DTE. It is used as a clock signal for DCE timing; a change in the signal line from ON to OFF indicates the centre of each bit of data on the line used to transmit from the DTE to the DCE – the Send Line.

It is similar in function to the Receive Timing signal line – pin 8.

Pin 18. Category II. Test Mode.

This line is controlled by the DCE. If the DCE turns this signal ON, it indicates to the DTE that the DCE is in a test condition, such as the loopback tests described previously. If the signal line is OFF, then it indicates that the DCE is in normal operation.

Pin 19. Signal Ground.

As with pin 7 of RS-232, this line is used is to connect together the circuit grounds of the DCE and DTE equipment.

Pin 20. Category II. Receive Common.

We now see an essential difference between RS-232 and RS-449. This signal line is used as a ground for the receive circuits of the DTE and DCE.

Pin 21. Spare pin.

There is now a general pairing of pins 22 onwards with pins 4 onwards described above (although not all corresponding pins are matched exactly). You will notice that the pins which pair up as having the same function are Category I pins only—a pair of connections are need for each of these, as they are the *differential category I circuits*.

Pin 4 & Pin 22	– Send Data.
Pin 5 & Pin 23	– Send Timing.
Pin 6 & Pin 24	– Receive Data.
Pin 7 & Pin 25	– Request To Send.
Pin 8 & Pin 26	– Receive Timing.
Pin 9 & Pin 27	– Clear To Send.
Pin 11 & Pin 29	– Data Mode.
Pin 12 & Pin 30	–Terminal Ready.
Pin 13 & Pin 31	– Receiver Ready.
Pin 17 & Pin 35	–Terminal Timing.

The remaining pins (necessarily Category II) are described below:

Pin 28. Terminal In Service.

Basically, when the DTE turns this line ON it is to indicate that the device is available for service.

Pin 32. Select Standby.

This signal line is controlled by the DTE. If the DTE turns this line ON, it indicates to the DCE that its standby communications facilities are requested.

Pin 33. Signal Quality.

The DCE will determine the state of this line. If the line is OFF, then the DCE is indicating that there is a high probability of error in the data on the Receive Data signal line; conversely, if ON, there is a low probability of error.

Pin 34. New Signal.

This signal line is used by the DTE to indicate to the DCE that it should be ready to respond to a new line signal.

Strictly speaking, when this signal line is ON the DCE should respond by turning OFF Receiver Ready, and set the Receive Data line to MARK.

When this line is then turned OFF, the DCE should be ready to respond to a new line signal - the New Signal line may be turned OFF any time after DCE has turned OFF the Receiver Ready line.

Pin 36. Standby Indicator.

This line is controlled by DCE, and offers the complementary function of Pin 32, the Select Standby line, described above. When ON, it indicates that the DCE is on standby with its communications facilities - if OFF, the the DCE is in its normal operating mode.

Pin 37. No Category. Send Common.

This is the common ground line for the Send circuits (see pin 20, Receive Common, above).

Finally, we consider the optional 9-pin D-type connector, which as you will probably remember is used for the secondary transmit/receive circuits.

All the following circuits (except for the shield line) are of Category II.

Pin 1. No Category. Shield.

As for pin 1 of the 37 pin D-type described previously, and the 25 pin D-type of the RS-232.

Pin 2. Secondary Receiver Ready.

This functions in the same way as Receiver Ready, which is pin 13 of the 37 pin connector.

Pin 3. Secondary Send Data.

As its name implies, this is the line used to transmit data on the secondary channel from DTE to DCE.

Pin 4. Secondary Receive Data.

Similarly, this is the line used to transmit to the DTE from the DCE.

Pin 5. Signal Ground.

As for pin 19 of the 37 pin connector.

Pin 6. Receive Common.

As for pin 20 of the 37 pin connector, but used for the secondary receive channel circuit.

Pin 7. Secondary Request To Send.

This is our familiar RTS line for the secondary channel.

Pin 8. Secondary Clear To Send.

This is the CTS line for our secondary channel.

Pin 9. Send Common.

As for pin 37 of the 37 pin connector.

Mechanical Specifications

As with the RS-232 interface standards, no strict guidelines are laid down for the connectors to be used in RS-449; however, the same type of connector, the D-type mentioned frequently above, are to be used. These are manufactured by Amphenol, Cannon and others.

As you will no doubt have realized by now, whereas the RS-232 utilizes just one 25 pin connector, the RS-449 specifies one 37 pin connector, and an optional 9 pin connector as well.

RS-449, then lays out the specifications for the signal lines and types of plugs to be used. In the next section we will consider the electrical specifications – RS-422 and RS-423.

Electrical Characteristics: RS-422 and RS-423

In the previous sections we have considered the alternative, upgraded communications standard to the RS-232. RS449 deals with the pin connections of our new connectors – but what of the electrical characteristics employed?

You will remember that the aim of the EIA has been to provide some degree of compatibility between RS-232 and any new standards laid down. However, since the overall aim is a radical upgrade in performance, which the old RS-232-type circuits could not hope to match, some differences have had to be incorporated in some of the circuit design to cope with this. This, it will have been seen, is the reason for some new circuits – using *balanced* lines. The electrical specifications for these are covered by RS-422-A; however, RS-232 utilizes *unbalanced* line circuits, and in order to still be compatible with this there is an alternative standard to RS422 – the RS-423-A.

What are the essential differences between balanced and unbalanced circuits?

Physically, a balanced circuit uses two signal lines for each signal element, whereas an unbalanced circuit uses just one, as well as just one signal ground line that is common to all signal lines.

Without delving into electrical circuit theory, the end result is that there are certain advantages of balanced lines over unbalanced. For instance, longer interconnection cables may be used. There are also advantages when considering *noise* – extraneous background signals which may be around (from other cables and devices, for instance).

We will give a brief outline of the electrical specifications laid down for the two standards.

RS-423-A

You will remember that the RS-232 specification required a line voltage of +3 to +25V for ON, and −3V to −25V for OFF. With the RS423, we now have the requirement of a line voltage for ON of between +4V and +6V; for OFF the requirement is naturally −4V to −6V. There is thus one immediate bonus of RS423 – the signal line voltages fit well into the range specified for RS-232.

Otherwise, the specification deals with electrical characteristics such as the capacitance of the interconnecting wires, the impedance of the line driver circuits and so forth.

Of more importance to us is the consequent increase possible in the length of interconnecting cable that can be used. You will probably recall that RS-232 is limited to 15 metres. Now, the length of cable that can be used is actually dependent on the baud rate being used for the transmission of data – the higher the baud rate, the shorter the maximum length of the cable. However, for the RS423, if a baud rate of, say, 9600 is used, then the interconnecting cable can be some 100 meters; for a baud rate of less than about 1200, the cable can be a maximum of 1000 metres.

RS-422-A

The voltage requirements for RS422 are that for an ON signal, the line should be at between +2V and +6V; similarly for OFF, between −2V and −6V. The balanced line circuits of RS-422 are necessarily more complex than the unbalanced lines of RS-232 and RS-423, and will consequently not be dealt with here indetail. However, the net result, and one of the most important things to the end user, is that the possible transmission distances are greatly increased. For a baud rate of anything less than about 100,000 a maximum length of about 1000 meters can be used; with a baud rate of 1 million, a length of 100 meters can be used; and for a baud rate of 10 million the maximum length of interconnecting cable is still over 10 meters.

There are thus already tremendous advantages over the RS-232!

CHAPTER 5

Handshaking

We have now examined, both in principle and in practice, some real communications systems. It should therefore be possible for us to now connect together two devices, using say their RS-232 ports, to transfer some data from one to the other, but we have to make sure of a number of things first. The wiring of the interconnecting leads, for instance, must be correct (remember – DTE to DCE and all that). We also need some sort of *communications package* to run on each of the devices. Of course if one is a printer, then that is all that it does in life. However, if the other one is a microcomputer, then we at least require some command (perhaps in the resident BASIC language) which allows us to print – like the LPRINT command you may be familiar with. But is there any other aspect of communications – and file transfer in particular – that we have not yet considered?

You will probably have not really known the purpose of all of the available pin connections in the RS-232 or RS-449. (From now on we will consider just the RS-232). You may remember, if you have read the descriptions, that most were concerned with controlling what was going on – telling the device at the other end of the interconnection what was happening. You should have recognized and remembered the three essential lines – transmit, receive, and ground – mind you!

However, consider what will happen in the real case of wanting to produce, say, a listing on a printer of a file of information we have on a microcomputer – perhaps a list of names and addresses. Let us first assume that we are able to connect up our micro to our printer successfully. Suppose we also have a command to output a file via the RS-232. If we invoke this command, what will the microcomputer do? It will go to look for the file we want to be printed, which will probably be on a diskette in one of the disk drives of the machine, read the records one by one and transmit them down the RS-232 line. What of the printer on the other end of the lead? It will accept the records one by one, probably temporarily storing them in an internal *buffer*, and then print them out.

No doubt everyone has seen a printer working at some time or another – they are quite slow machines. At best, a desktop printer may print at around 160 characters per second (cps); or for cheaper printers this may be 80-100 cps.

For letter quality printers, the speed may be much slower – perhaps 30 to 40 cps. Now, it is quite obvious that a microcomputer is capable of churning out characters from a file much faster than a printer can print them. But how is this to be regulated?

This is where the concept of *handshaking* comes in. We require a system that allows the printer to tell the microcomputer "hang on a minute – I'm getting full", and then later say "it's o.k. now – you can send me some more records".

There are two possible ways for us to do this. We could have special *control codes* which the printer sends to the microcomputer, along one of the transmit/receive lines, that tell the micro what to do. This is called *software handshaking* – the handshaking is done by the computer program, or software, which runs the whole show. Alternatively, as you have probably guessed already from the specifications laid out for the RS-232, we could use one or more of the extra signal lines to say what was going on – perhaps ON for GO, OFF for STOP. This is called *hardware handshaking* – the handshaking is controlled by the the electronic circuits, or hardware.

5.1 Software Handshaking – XON/XOFF

Software handshaking has the advantage that fewer signal lines are required – normally just the transmit, receive and ground lines are needed in fact. As mentioned above, the principle behind software handshaking is that control codes, which are special codes that either device can recognize as signalling something of note, are sent along with the normal stream of data records from one device to another to control the flow of data. What are these control characters? You will remember that we are using the ASCII code for translation from our alphanumeric characters to the bytes to be transmitted, and then from the received bytes back to everyday symbols again. Now, not all of the ASCII table is used up by letters (both lower and upper case) and numbers, for all of our letters and numbers occupy the range from 20 hexadecimal (i.e. 32 decimal) upwards. Everything below (but not including) 20 hex is a control code, as well as 7F hex, which is the code for DELETE. It is these codes which help to control what is going on – on the screen of a monitor for instance. You will no doubt recognize familiar codes such as CARRIAGE RETURN, and LINEFEED. Now. any customized system could be set up by anybody for a software handshaking system, but this would not fit in well with our ideals of standardization across a range of systems. However, the most common form of software handshaking uses two particular control codes, known as Device Control 1 (DC1) and Device Control 3 (DC3), otherwise known as XON and XOFF.

The principle of XON/XOFF handshaking is easy. Suppose, again, that we have a microcomputer sending records one by one to a printer. The microcomputer, as well as sending records along the TRANSMIT line, can monitor the RECEIVE line to see if the printer is sending anything back to it. If the microcomputer receives a byte of data which is 13H (hexadecimal), i.e. DC3 or XOFF, it recognizes that the printer is telling it to wait for a time. The microcomputer will now stop sending any more records; it will simply sit there, continually waiting for anything on the receive line. It is only when it duly receives 11H, i.e. DC1 or XON, that it will start sending data again. Easy, isn't it?

From the printer's point of view, all it has to do is to receive the records one by one and print them out, to the best of its ability. If the records are being sent down too fast, it simply has to transmit to the microcomputer an XOFF; then, when it has cleared the backlog of data to be printed, it sends an XON to indicate that it is ready to receive again.

Of course, we need not restrict ourselves to the situation of a computer connected to a printer, with data going only one way. This principle can be extended to two-way conversation between computers; here of course is the advantage of using distinct control characters – they cannot be confused with our text data, although they may be transmitted in the same string of data.

The fundamental requirement for software handshaking is that the receiving machine *must be capable of transmitting characters as well*. This may not always be the case; some printers for instance may have the electronic circuitry to receive only. In these cases, we must use *hardware handshaking*.

5.2 Hardware Handshaking – RTS/CTS.

Consider the case of two computers connected together; we may require one to transfer a file to another, or there may be an interactive conversation going on between the two. In either case, if we are to use hardware handshaking, (that is, using extra signal lines), we require one line with which the DTE tells the DCE what to do, and another line for the DCE to tell the DTE what to do. From the specification laid down for RS-232, the usual and most common lines to use are pins 4 and 5 – the Request To Send (RTS) and Clear To Send (CTS) signal lines. The DTE tells the DCE what to do by means of the RTS line; conversely, the DCE tells the DTE what to do by means of the CTS line.

Their functioning is again quite straightforward. Suppose we first consider the DCE sending a file of data to the DTE. By the specifications laid down, the DCE should first make sure that its CTS line is held *high*. It then starts to transmit its file to the DTE. Now, before it sends each character in turn down the

RS-232 it should look at the RTS line – if this is HIGH, then all is well and another character can be transmitted. However, if the DTE has pulled its RTS line LOW, then the DCE knows it must wait before sending the next character. It simply waits in a loop, checking the RTS line continuously to see if it has gone back to HIGH. When it has, it knows that it can send the next character.

The CTS line works in exactly the same way for controlling data transfer from the DTE to the DCE. The DTE has to continually check the CTS line to see what state it is in, and sends another character or waits accordingly.

RTS/CTS is the most common type of hardware handshaking. However, you will no doubt be aware that there are plenty of other signal lines available on our 25 pin RS-232 – some of the others must be used for something! In fact, there are a few other common hardware handshake lines, such as DSR, DTR, and DCD. These lines, though, tend to be used not for character-by-character handshaking, but for overall state of readiness signal. Thus, whilst it may be necessary to have these lines wired up correctly, they may only be ON or OFF depending on whether or not the machine is turned on or off. Of course, their correct functioning may still be crucial to the whole communications system; there are ways to cheat, which will be explained in a later chapter!

What, then, are the advantages and disadvantages of these two fundamentally different systems? Software handshaking requires both transmit and receive capability – our devices may not be able to cope with this. Hardware handshaking, on the other hand, requires two extra control lines. If we are to have cables over a long distance, this may not be desirable. Indeed, hardware handshaking is not possible at all when transmitting over telephone lines by using a modem or acoustic coupler – in this case software handshaking *must* be used.

Generally, most devices nowadays are capable of dealing with both types of handshaking; there is usually little advantage in one or another. It is down to personal preference when there is a choice.

CHAPTER 6

Communications Packages

We have now considered everything we need to know, in theory, to be able to connect together two pieces of machinery with RS-232-C interfaces; we should be able to hook up transmit lines, receive lines, and handshaking lines. But this is not enough!

One common mistake the layman makes is to think that once the rather confusing subject of actually wiring up an RS-232 has been mastered, then everything else that he wants to happen will magically do so. Unfortunately there is now a second (but final, fortunately) stumbling block to be overcome. We may have a lead plugged into the back of our computer, but so what? The computer probably could not care less, and will quite willingly ignore this port unless instructed otherwise. What is required is some *communications software* to run the whole show.

If we are lucky, any communications software that we require for our task may be included already in the machine. For instance, consider the common case of our requiring to produce a listing of a file on a printer. Then we require two pieces of communications software – one in the printer, and one in our host computer device. Naturally, the manufacturers of the printer will have included in the machine all the software to make the machine run – its only purpose in life is to produce printouts, after all. Also, most computer manufacturers will provide, in the *operating system*, some way of producing a listing. This may be by an LPRINT command in the BASIC language, for instance. Or there may be a series of keypresses, or setup system, to redirect the output *from* the screen *to* the RS-232. Thus everything that used to be displayed on the screen will now, instead, be transmitted down the RS-232.

This is the simple case of producing a listing on a printer, but what of other situations? For instance, we may wish to connect together two microcomputers to transfer a file from one to the other. Or we may have our microcomputer connected up to a modem and telephone line; perhaps we wish to log on to an electronic mail system such as Telecom Gold, or Easylink. We might even wish to connect our micro up to a powerful supermini or mainframe computer, and use it merely as a dumb terminal. We obviously require something more sophisticated to deal with these situations.

6.1 What is needed?

We now see the need for a communications package – something that will take over control of our machine, and convert its functioning into an adaptable, useful tool for communicating with the outside world.

But what features will we require of this package? You will recall that, before any communications actually takes place, everything needs to be set up correctly – for instance the *baud rate* and *handshaking*. There are thus usually two distinct sides to a communications package (normally abbreviated to "comms package"): on the one hand, we need to have our send and receive functions, whilst on the other hand we need to be able to configure our system for a variety of needs.

Different communications packages for different machines differ in their exact specifications, but there is a minimum requirement for any effective package. Suppose the package does not allow us to alter, say, the baud rate, and this is fixed at 9600. Now, we may have a printer which also has a fixed baud rate – this might be 1200. There is no way that we will be able to get one to communicate with the other – but which should be the more flexible of the two? Presumably this should be our computer, since it will have greater processing power than the printer. Fortunately, in practice, communications packages allow us to configure the system to produce a wide variety of settings, to cope with the equally wide variety of situations that we might come across in the future.

What is the minimum to expect from a communications package? There will normally be some sort of *configuration*, or *setup* procedure. This should allow you to alter:

    BAUD RATE
    PARITY
    STOP BITS
    DATA BITS
    HANDSHAKING

at the very least.

Baud Rate

The baud rate should normally be configurable in the range 150-9600 baud. The normal steps to use are:

    150, 300, 600, 1200, 2400, 4800, 9600.

You may also see the lower baud rates of 50, 75, and 110.Note that 75 is essential if the older type of split baud rate (i.e. 1200/75) telephone links are to be used.

You may also see the higher rate of 19200 baud – although beware, as on most machines this, rather like car speedometers, is a bit of an exaggeration and usually most unreliable.

The other baud rates you may come across, with more sophisticated packages, are:

134.5, 200, 1800, and 2000.

Parity

The minimum choices for parity should be:

NONE, ODD, EVEN.

You may also see the extra choices

MARK and SPACE.

Stop Bits

Normally the choice, if any, is between

1 STOP BIT or 2 STOP BITS.

It may be the case that just one stop bit is normally sent, unless a very low baud rate of, say, 150 or lower is selected; in this case the software may automatically assume that 2 stop bits should be sent.

There is also sometimes the rather unusual choice of ONE AND A HALF STOP BITS! This curious case arises, historically, from early machines which, it was found, needed longer than the length of time that just one stop bit was present on the transmit/receive line in order to detect what was going on; however, sending two stop bits, whilst certainly solving the problem, was thought to waste rather too much time. Thus the solution was to hold the stop bit value on the line for one and a half times as long as usual. Nowadays, it is not generally thought worth the extra effort required in (usually) the hardware design of the Serial I/O chip to cater for this possibility.

Data Bits

One would always expect the choice to be between

7 DATA BITS or 8 DATA BITS

to be able to cope with 7 bit ASCII, or full 8 bit binary data.

You may sometimes see the additional choices of 5 or 6 data bits, but these are rarely used.

Handshaking

Any device should offer some sort of handshaking, for without this there is little hope (unless you write your own handshaking program) of successful file transfer.

Having said that, there are still times when it is advantageous to be able to disable the handshaking – perhaps in initial testing stages. Thus the choice is normally between:

NONE and XON/XOFF (i.e. software handshaking) or

NONE and RTS/CTS (i.e. hardware handshaking),

or, if the machine is capable of it, between all three:

NONE, RTS/CTS, or XON/XOFF.

What other features are there that we might require?

Consider, for example, our problem of printing out the contents of a file. Now, this file will consist of a number of records, saved one after the other. Our printing program will thus read successive data records, and send them one by one to the printer. How will the printer know when one record ends, and another one starts? What is required is some kind of *end of line marker*. The usual method is by using another of our CONTROL CODES – in this case the familiar CARRIAGE RETURN code. This is probably familiar to most of us as the RETURN key on a keyboard – it simply returns the cursor back to its leftmost position on the screen, at the start of a line. It derives its name from typewriters, where the paper carriage mechanism has to be returned to its leftmost position at the end of every line. The typing pool of secretaries and dinging bells from typewriters has long gone, but the name still remains!

In ASCII, a carriage return is signified by the control code which has a value of 0D hexadecimal, or 13 in decimal.

Thus, our microcomputer will, at the end of every record, and thus every line, of data, send a carriage return (CR for short) to the printer. The printer will then duly return to the start of the line. But what if we now just send down the next record? The printer will simply print over the line of data it has just printed out – we are still on the same line!

Hence the need for another control code – LINE FEED (LF). As its name clearly implies, it acts simply to instruct a device to go on to a new line. Looking at the table of ASCII characters, you will see that line feed is 0A hex, or 10 decimal.

Thus we require our END OF LINE definition to be set to Carriage Return, and then Line Feed.

Without wishing to confuse the issue, this may not always be necessary. For instance, most printers can also be configured to a certain extent – baud rate, parity etc. They may also give you the option of setting them to AUTO LINEFEED. In this case, when the printer receives a carriage return, it will automatically assume that a line feed is required afterwards as well. In this case we clearly need our end of line definition to be just carriage return – unless, that is, we want a blank line in between each record.

We may not require a line feed after every carriage return in other circumstances – for instance if we are talking to a host computer system, such as a minicomputer or mainframe, or to a mainframe computer via the telephone lines. In this case a carriage return is normally all that is required.

Another common choice in setting up a communications system is that of ECHO. You may also see the choices of LOCAL ECHO, or HOST ECHO, or similar. What does all this mean?

Normally, when using a communications package, if you press a key on the keyboard of your device, two things will happen: the keypress will result in a character being displayed on the screen of the VDU, and the character will be sent down the RS-232. This is LOCAL ECHO; your machines controls the process of putting the character you have pressed onto the screen.

There is an alternative, which is generally used when connecting a terminal up to a HOST computer. In this system, called HOST ECHO, a keypress on the keyboard results only in the corresponding character being sent down the RS-232 line – nothing is put onto your VDU screen. However, when the host machine receives the character, it ECHOES it back to you down its transmit line, or your receive line. You thus duly recognize this as a character from the host machine – not necessarily knowing whether it is one of your characters, or one originating from the host. There is normally no noticeable time lag between pressing a key and seeing it appear on the screen – certainly at 9600 baud, and usually at such low speeds as 300 baud.

Note that there is no danger if you are inadvertantly set to LOCAL ECHO instead of HOST ECHO but eevveerryytthhiinngg wwiillll bbee rreeppeeaatteedd ttwwiiccee oonn tthhee ssccrreeeenn!!

6.2 Choosing a Communications Package.

We have thus considered the setup, or configuration, system. This is just one half of our communications system – more important to us is how to actually get things moving along the lines!

We will probably have different requirements for different situations. There may be no need to have a full-blown, and expensive, *terminal emulation* package (more on this in the next section) if we require only simple file transfer, or printing functions. On the other hand, we may wish to talk to a computer system via the telephone network which is on the other side of the world, and have "autoanswer" facilities should any other computer system try to contact us. You will thus have to give careful consideration to the type of functions you require, and your budget.

Hopefully you may actually have got just what you require when you bought your computer system – if you just require the ability to produce listings, then your computer can probably do this quite easily already. Any wordprocessor, database or graphics package for instance, should also include the ability to produce listings. If you require simple file transfer, then not much programming ability is necessarily required (though perhaps quite a lot of time "debugging"!) to write your own simple system using whatever species of BASIC language is included with your machine – there is guidance on this matter in a later chapter.

Let us in the next section consider the idea of *terminal emulation* – a microcomputer pretending to be a terminal.

6.3 Terminal Emulation

We now come to a particular type of communications package – a terminal emulation program. What is this?

A terminal is a device quite distinct from a desktop microcomputer. Its function is to provide a means of communication with a computer. As such, it probably will not be much use on its own – it will not be capable of being used like a microcomputer. Thus, you will not be able to write and run programs on it; you will not be able to play video games on it either!

Whereas a desktop microcomputer has its own microprocessor for running programs, and probably one or more disk drive units as well, a terminal has to derive all of its processing power from the host computer. Indeed, this host computer, which may be a minicomputer (nowadays often called a "supermini", as many desktop microcomputers have the same processing power as a minicomputer of just a few years ago) or a mainframe computer, will be servicing many terminals at once; perhaps several dozen.

A desktop microcomputer can thus be regarded as an all-in-one system – a processing black box with a built-in terminal. There are times, however, when we may wish our microcomputer to actually be a terminal. For instance, we may wish to generally use its stand-alone functions, such as wordprocessing, on our desktop (perhaps with security of data in mind). Now, our workplace may also boast a powerful computer system, which we may wish to "log in" to sometimes. Rather than have a separate terminal on our desktop as well, which will waste both space and money, we may wish to connect our microcomputer into the host computer instead.

Basic Concepts

Let us consider what we require of a terminal.

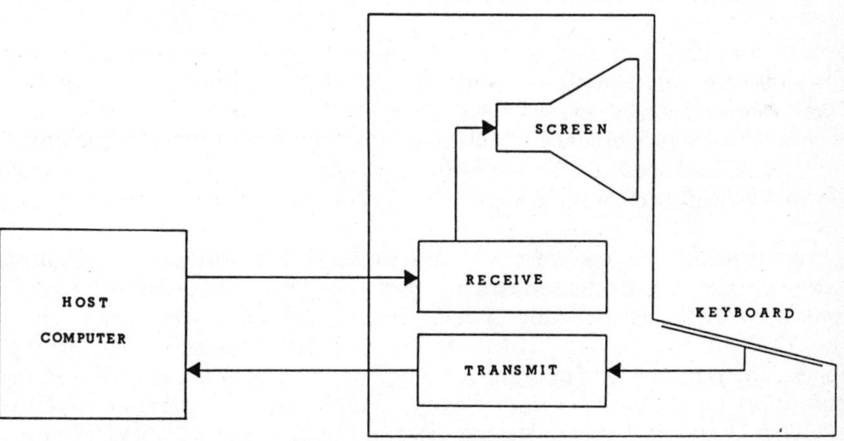

Fig. 6.1 An On-line terminal.

You will notice that our representation of a terminal on-line illustrates the concept of host echo; there is no connection from the keyboard input to the screen output, except by going via the host computer. This situation does not arise when the terminal is off-line: now the characters typed in on the keyboard appear directly on the screen. In this case, there is no direct connection from the transmit and receive functions to the host computer; instead, the output from the transmit is connected directlyto the input of the receive. (*Local echo* is a combinationof the two—characters typed in at the keyboard are both transmitted to the host computer, and also redirected to the receive function of the terminal).

How does our terminal differ from a microcomputer? As we noted above, a terminal will only do what its host computer tells it to do. When we turn on the terminal, and before we press any keys, the screen will probably stay totally blank. Compare this with turning on your microcomputer—there will probably be an opening message, stating the machine type and so on. You may well be greeted by an infuriating wait while the machine performs a "RAM check". If the microcomputer is of the home variety, such as an Atari or an Acorn, it will probably go straight into the BASIC language, in which case you will probably be welcomed by the message READY. If, however, it goes into a more esoteric operating system, you will probably see something like

```
A>
```

appear on the screen.

Nothing like this will happen with a terminal, until you press a key—normally a carriage return or two is required to alert the host computer you are connected to that something is going on.

From now on, the terminal emulation system is simple—the terminal is under the entire control of the host computer; it hardly has to think for itself. Thus each character typed in on the keyboard will be transmitted to the host computer; strings of characters will not be interpreted. Any interpretation of the instructions will be done by the host computer; any messages sent back will simply be displayed on the screen.

There are many different types of terminals available for different applications and environments, although there are just a few standard types whose features and specification are generally copied. One of IBM's standard terminal types is the 3270—remember that IBM use the EBCDIC character set for their mainframe computers. The standard range of terminals for use with ASCII is generally regarded as being Digital Equipment Corporation's (DEC) VT52/VT100 series. There are others, such as the Zenith Z19/Z29 VDU, and so on. But what else is there to consider in the functioning of a terminal that might produce differences? One additional point to consider is how a terminal copes with cursor positioning (or how to move the little blob around on the screen), and text editing – how to erase a line, or quit from a command that has been submitted.

Let us view some of the common control codes (a few of which we have already discussed), and so-called *escape sequences*. You will recognize most codes from the ASCII character table.

07H (7 Decimal) Bell (BEL)

This control code sounds a bleep.

08H (8 Decimal) Backspace (BS)

Moves the cursor left one position. If auto-wrap is enabled, and the cursor is is in the leftmost column of any line apart from the top one, then it is moved to the rightmost column of the row above.

09H (9 Decimal) Horizontal Tab (HT)

This moves the cursor to the next tab stop, or to the rightmost column if there are no more tab stops.

0AH (10 Decimal) Linefeed (LF)

Move the cursor down one line. Under certain circumstances the background will instead scroll up one line.

0BH (11 Decimal) Vertical Tab (VT)

Generally processed as a linefeed.

0CH (12 Decimal) Form Feed (FF)

A terminal will generally process this as a linefeed, although note that a printer would throw onto a new form (usually the start of a page).

0DH (13 Decimal) Carriage Return (CR)

This serves to move the cursor to the leftmost column of the current row.

11H (17 Decimal) Device Control 1 (DC1 – or XON)

Terminals usually operate in XON/XOFF handshaking mode. This control code tells the terminal to carry on transmitting characters.

13H (19 Decimal) Device Control 3 (DC3 – or XOFF)

This will tell the terminal to stop transmitting characters (except XON's and XOFF's).

1BH (27 decimal) Escape (ESC)

This introduces an *escape sequence*.

Escape and Control Sequences

You will remember from the ASCII Character Table that there is room for only about 32 control codes – codes we can use to tell a particular device what to do. This space is obviously easily exhausted, as there are many possible uses for control codes. To overcome this limitation, a *sequence* of control codes can be sent, and interpreted by our terminal. These sequences are usually preceded by an ESC code. We can thus, in possibly just two characters (ESC + extra character), instruct our terminal to perform editing features such as delete a line, delete a character, or move the cursor to a given position.

Note that an ESCAPE SEQUENCE is defined as:

ESC	I...I	F1
Escape sequence introducer	Intermediate characters (0 or more)	One Final character

whilst a CONTROL SEQUENCE is defined as:

CSI	P...P	I...I	F2
Control sequence introducer (same as ESC)	Parameter characters (0 or more)	Intermediate characters (0 or more)	One Final character

ESC is 1BH (27 Decimal), as stated above.

Parameter characters are in the range 30H – 3FH
(48 – 63 decimal) i.e.
0, 1, „, , >, ?

Intermediate characters are in the range 20H – 2FH
(32 – 47 decimal) i.e.
space, !, „, , ., /

For an escape sequence, the final character F1 is in the range

   30H − 7EH (48 − 126 decimal)

whilst for a control sequence, the final character F2 is in the range

   40H − 7EH (64 − 126 decimal).

Examples of Escape Sequences

ESC A	Cursor up. If already at the top, do nothing.
ESC B	Cursor down. If at the bottom, do nothing.
ESC C	Cursor right. If in rightmost column, do nothing.
ESC D	Cursor left. If in leftmost column, do nothing.
ESC H	Move cursor to HOME (top left hand corner).
ESC L	Insert a line. All the rows below and including the cursor line are scrolled down; the cursor rowis cleared, and the cursor position is unaffected.
ESC N	Delete the character at the cursor position. All characters to the right of the cursor are moved one place to the left – the leftmost position is cleared.
ESC [? 4 h	Set smooth scroll mode.

There are, of course, many other escape sequences in common usage; these will be dependent on the type of terminal actually being used. The exact escape sequences should be documented for the terminal in question.

CHAPTER 7

Writing a Communications Package for the RS-232

In previous chapters we have considered the hardware arrangements of actually wiring up one device to another, and some of the software needs: communications software, a terminal emulation package, and a terminal itself. However, whilst most of us will be quite happy to pay the (rather exorbitant) price of buying from a shop both the hardware (an interconnecting lead) and the software (a communications package for example), the bold-hearted may wish to have a go at wiring up an interconnecting lead, or indeed writing some communications software themselves. In later chapters we will consider how to go about successfully wiring one device to another, with particular reference to some everyday microcomputers and printers.

In this chapter, however, we will consider some of the fundamentals of communications software. We will look at two different aspects – writing a simple file transfer program in a particular dialect of the Basic programming language, and writing low-level communications software for simple character, and thus file, transfer, in a particular assembler language. In this latter case we will also consider elements of handshaking, both hardware and software.

7.1 General Ideas

What do we require in principle for our file transfer program? We can break the logic down into a number of simple steps, which can be represented by a flow chart.

A flow chart may be most useful for illustrating program logic and design in textbooks and in the classroom. However, in practice you will find that the device is never used by the hardened software engineer, or indeed any hacker, worth his or her salt! Nevertheless, we shall for the moment stick by this useless device.

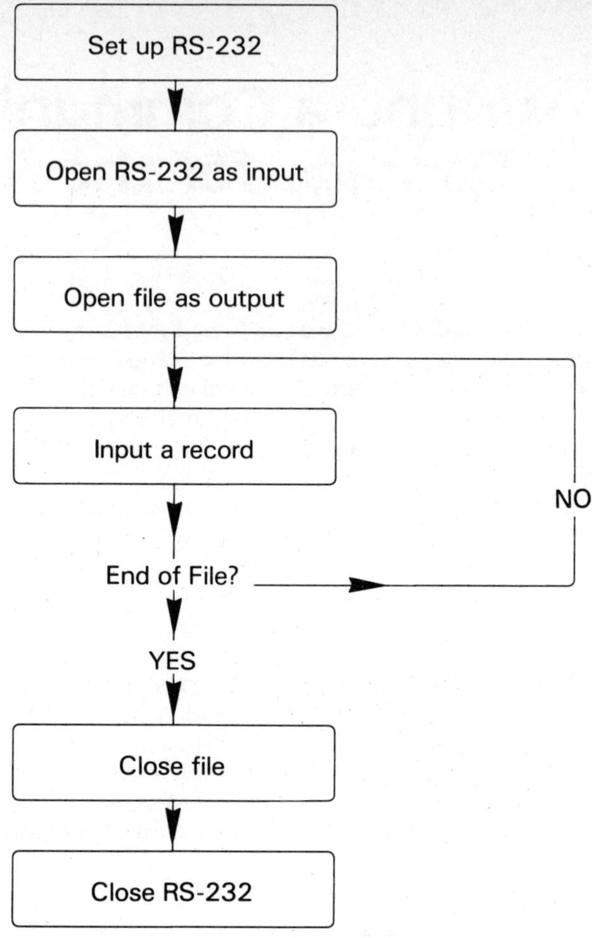

Fig. 7.1 Transmitting from device to us

Seems simple, doesn't it? This may not always be true in practice!

For file transfer the other way — *from* our device *to* a target machine, the roles of the RS-232 port and file are reversed — the RS-232 becomes the output, and the file is the input.

Note that we could also consider the problem of character by-character transfer, instead of record-by-record, as above. In this case, instead of the logic box

we have

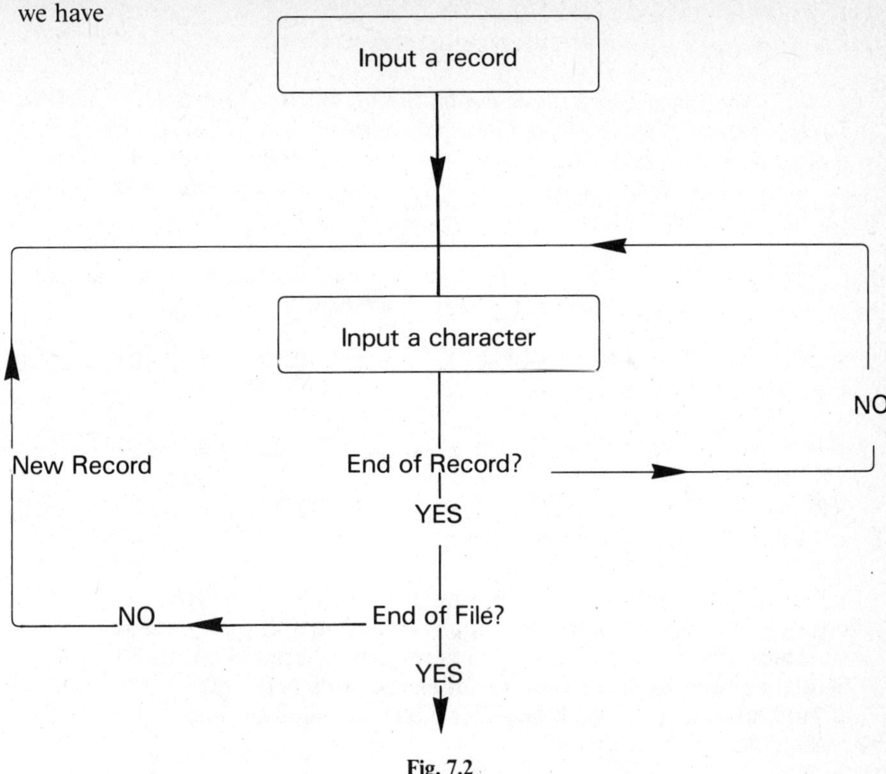

Fig. 7.2

Whether we have to take this course depends on the capabilities of the language we are using; i.e. to what extent it can handle records and files itself, without too much assistance.

7.2 An Example in BASIC, on the IBM PC

Let us now see how to embody these ideas into a working system. The IBM has a number of powerful BASIC languages available, such as BASICA and GWBasic (Gee Wizz Basic!).

Whilst it is impossible, in giving examples, to cater for every possible taste and eventuality, the following programs should serve to give, if not an exact working piece of software, then at least firm guidelines to follow.

Consider, first, our RS-232 port. The IBM family of PC's, and its compatible machines, have a number of expansion slots in the back of the casing. One of these is normally assigned to a plug-in board which is the RS-232 interface. This is usually assigned to com1: the communications port 1.

The BASIC language has a mode command to configure the RS-232 port for baud rate, parity, number of data bits, and number of stop bits, as you should expect by now. This is not a complex, sophisticated setup system, as might be found in communications packages, but it is quite sufficient to set up the RS-232 port as required.

For instance, we might require 1200 baud, no parity, eight data bits, and one stop bit. In this case the first line of our program will be:

```
10 OPEN "COM1:1200,N,8,1,CS10000,DS10000" FOR
INPUT AS #3
```

If we require the RS-232 port to be the output, then line 10 will be:

```
10 OPEN "COM1:1200,N,8,1,CS10000,DS10000" FOR
OUTPUT AS #3
```

Most of the parameters in line 10 are straightforward. Note the last two, though. These are *timeout* parameters. For suppose that something goes wrong with our communications system; if our IBM is receiving, it may be sitting in a loop, patiently waiting for some kind of input. But this may never come, so if we configure the system to break out after a certain length of time, or timeout, we have a chance of recovery.

Our parameters can range from 0 to 65535. Note that the maximum value is the maximum for an unsigned two byte integer – i.e. 2^{16}.

We might now wish to prompt the user to enter a filename to be used, for instance

```
30 LINE INPUT "File Name?";FILE$
```

and then open this file for either output or input, depending on which way the file transfer is to take place.

So we might have

```
40 OPEN FILE$ FOR INPUT AS #2
```

or

```
40 OPEN FILE$ FOR OUTPUT AS #2
```

You will see that we are assigning the RS-232 port and the file to one of two CHANNELS – channel number 2, i.e #2, and channel number 3, i.e. #3.

Suppose then we wish to transfer from an external device to the IBM PC. Our RS-232 will thus be set up as input, and our file as output. We may wish to receive the whole file into the microcomputer before saving it, to a file on disk for instance. In this case we will need to reserve an area of memory for our file. This can be done by setting up an ARRAY, and denoting a certain space, or DIMENSION, for it.

i.e.

```
50 DIM ARRAY$(1024)
```

In this case we are reserving 1024 bytes, or 1 kilobyte (1K, that is, 2^{10}, which is roughly 1000) for our file save area. We may require more – in which case more space can be alloted (depending on the configuration, and therefore maximum RAM size, of our system).

We now set up a counter to keep track of the records as they are input one by one. This must first be initialized to zero, for instance

```
60 X=0
```

There is one more item to be considered before embarking upon receiving a file – how do we know when we have reached the end? You will probably remember that there is a particular control code which is generally reserved for this use – End Of File (EOF). This has the value 1A hexadecimal (26 decimal). So we can define a string variable as this end of file character, i.e.

```
70 EOF$=CHR$(26)
```

which gives us a reference character to check for.

We can now construct the main program loop, which will receive records one by one, and save them in our temporary storage area.

First, our line to increment our record count, for each new record

```
100 X=X+1
```

Next, receive a record from the RS-232, and save it in our array

```
110 INPUT #3,ARRAY$(X)
```

Thus our first record will be in the first element of our array, the second record in our second element, and so on.

We may now wish to print out on the screen of the IBM each record as it is received. This can be accomplished by

```
120 PRINT ARRAY$(X)
```

Finally, we check to see if our last received record was in fact an end of file marker. If it was not, we can go back to receive another record:

```
130 IF ARRAY(X)<>EOF$ THEN 100
```

We now have the received file in memory. All we have to do is to write the records, one by one, to our file on disk. This can be achieved by a simple loop:

```
140 FOR Y=1 TO X
150 PRINT #2, ARRAY=(X)
160 NEXT Y
```

Note that in line 150 we use the PRINT command, as when actually listing out to the screen, but this time the output is redirected to a new output stream: the open file on disk.

Suppose that we now wish to do the converse; that is, to read a file we already have on a disk, and transmit the records one by one down the RS-232 interface to some receiving device. Our first steps will of course be to open the RS-232 as OUTPUT, and the file as INPUT, as described above. We then set up a simple loop to read records one by one from the open file, and print them, perhaps to the screen as we go along, but also to the RS-232 output. Note that in line 230 we check to see if an End-Of-File marker has been received from the file; if so, we quit out of the program loop.

```
200 INPUT #2,ARRAY$
210 PRINT ARRAY$
220 PRINT #3,ARRAY$
230 IF NOT EOF(2) THEN 200
```

We may now wish to send an EOF marker to our receiving device; otherwise, it will not know either when the last record has been received!

```
240 PRINT #3,EOF$
```

Finally, all that remains to be done in either case is to close off both files:

```
250 CLOSE 2
260 CLOSE 3
999 END
```

There are a number of points to born in mind with the above program. First, of course, is the actual syntax of the BASIC dialect you are using (and, indeed, just how it handles the RS-232 port and file handling). Second, is the handshaking. The IBM automatically supports hardware handshaking, using the RTS and CTS lines, as is usual. You should thus make sure that you have wired up these lines correctly in your interconnecting lead, and also that your receiving device can, itself, hardware handshake.

Finally, the speed that the BASIC runs at may determine how fast your file transfer can be (i.e. the maximum permitted baud rate); it may be necessary, indeed, to take steps to speed up the BASIC program, by for instance writing multiple commands on one line in crucial program loops.

7.3 An Example in Assembler language, based on the Hitachi 6800 Series of Microprocessors

Hitachi of Japan produce a range of microprocessors based on the successful Motorola 6800 series. The range includes, for example, the HD6803, an 8-bit NMOS microprocessor which is compatible with the MC6803 and MC6803-1, and also the HD6303, a CMOS version of the NMOS one.

(Without wishing to delve into too much detail over microprocessor design, NMOS and CMOS chips differ in their design and construction. The end result is that CMOS chips consume less power – making them more suitable when the power supply is limited, for instance in hand-held battery operated systems.)

We will consider assembler language software development using this family of chips as an example, although the principles developed can of course be applied to any particular microprocessor configuration, given that the hardware is suitable for serial communications.

This family of Hitachi chips is well suited to communications development. It is compatible with the Motorola range of equivalent microprocessors, and has some extra features thrown in for good measure. Thus the microprocessor units (MPU's) are *object code* compatible (the object code is the raw, final, code that MPU's actually run on and understand); there are also improvements in execution of some instructions, and extra on-board hardware features. Not least important of these, for our purposes, is the inclusion of an on-chip Serial Communications Interface (SCI) – effectively a built-in RS-232! The SCI is, furthermore, most flexible in that it can equally well be configured as a *clocked synchronous* communications device.

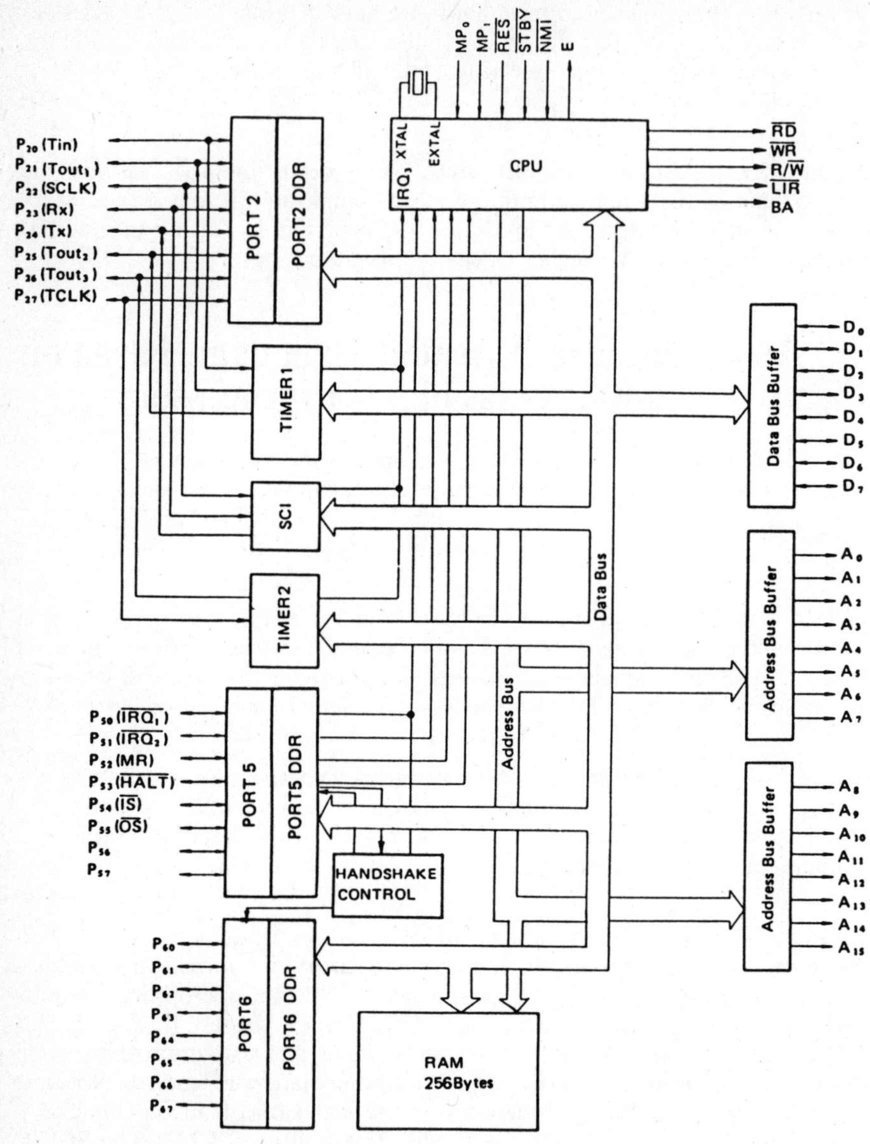

Fig. 7.3 Block Diagram of HD6303X

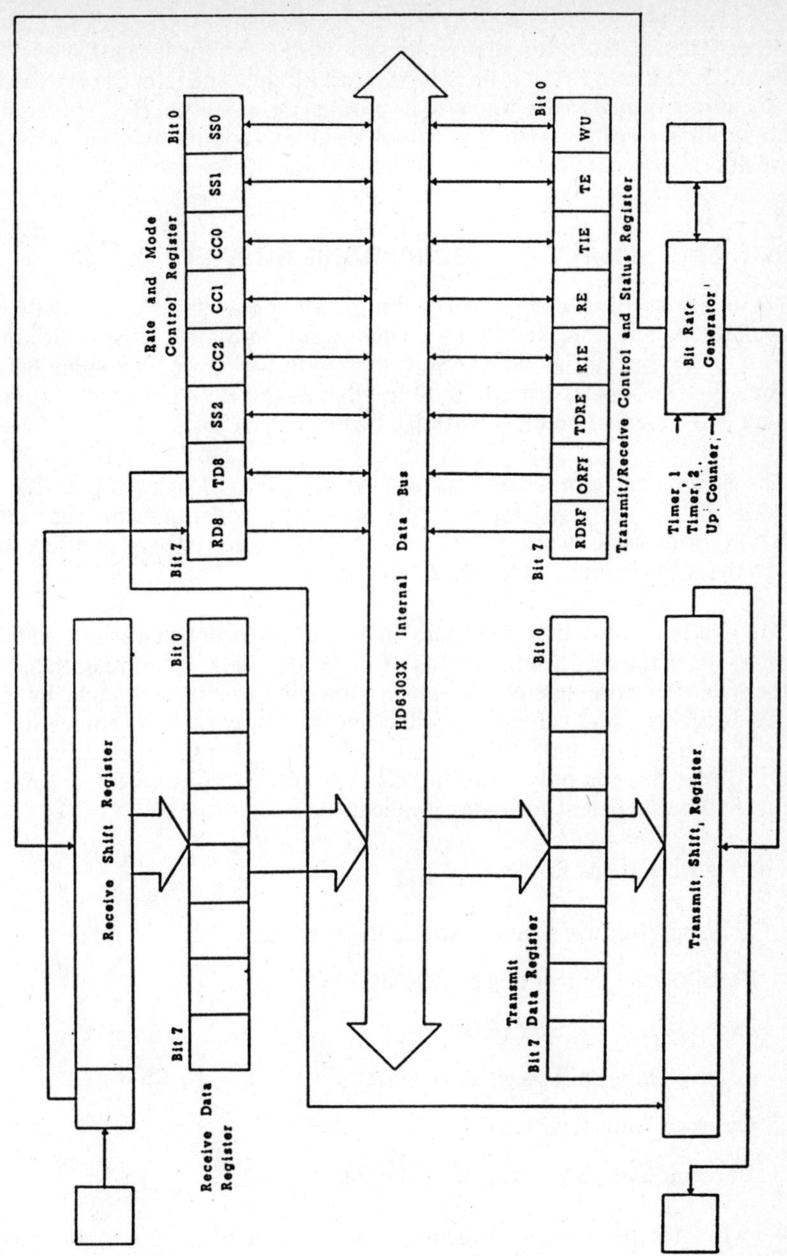

Fig. 7.4 SCI Block Diagram

69

In particular, we will use as reference the Hitachi HD6303X MPU. Amongst other features, in common with the rest of the family, it has 192 bytes of on-board RAM, two timers (one programmable, and one reloadable), the built-in SCI as mentioned above, and also 24 parallel input/output (I/O) ports. It is with these ports, as will be seen, that we will be able to communicate with the outside world.

7.4 The Serial Communications Interface (SCI)

Let us first consider the Serial Communications Interface. There are two modes available when using the SCI – asynchronous and clocked synchronous. The former can be configured as one system with which we have some familiarity already – the RS-232 (or compatible, such as the RS-423). In the latter mode, data can be transferred synchronized with a serial clock.

Ths SCI has a number of *registers*, which are used to configure the system initially. These registers are all one byte locations in the on-board RAM – moreover, they are all in ZERO PAGE. Zero page is, in effect, the first 256 bytes of memory, starting from zero.

You will remember that our basic unit used in storing characters, transferring data, etc. is the *byte*. This consists of eight bits. Now, we have in the past used the byte as a complete entity – always lumping together all eight bytes. With these registers, and others you will come across, each *bit* becomes significant itself. You will see that distinct bits of a byte are used to indicate distinct states. Of course, this can only be a simple state – either ON or OFF (i.e. 1 or 0) – but this will be sufficient for many applications.

The registers are as follows:

Transmit/Receive Control Status Register (TRCSR)

Rate/Mode Control Register (RMCR)

Receive Data Register (RDR)

Receive Data Shift Register (RDSR)

Transmit Data Register (TDR)

Transmit Data Shift Register (TDSR)

We will later also have to consider the use of one of the internal timers of the microprocessor. This will be used, in effect, to provide the timing for our selected baud rate.

Let us, for the moment, return to consideration of the SCI. You will notice that most of the registers are to do with our familiar feature of Transmit and Receive functions. In fact, we need not concern ourselves too much with these – their operation is either straightforward in use, or will not concern us at all. They will be considered in detail later; but first, we come to perhaps the two most important registers – the Transmit/Receive Control Status Register, and the Rate and Mode Control Register.

The Transmit/Receive Control Status Register

Bit number

7	6	5	4	3	2	1	0
RDRF	ORFE	TDRE	RIE	RE	TIE	TE	WU

Fig. 7.5 TRCSR

Notice that, in a byte, the bits are numbered 0 – 7; that is, least significant bit up to most significant bit, or right to left.

Let us examine the bits one by one.

Bit 0. Wake-up (WU)

As its name implies, this bit is set or cleared to utilize or inhibit a "wake-up" feature of the microprocessor unit. We will not be using this feature in this example – thus the bit should be set to 0. However, if set to 1, its function is to wait for a string of 10 or 11 consecutive "1" bits. On receiving this string, the MPU wakes up, clears this bit, and starts receiving again. Before this, the MPU will have been ignoring any received bits of data.

Its use lies in enabling the microprocessor to ignore, and hence not have to process, any information that will be uninteresting to it, until such time as there is interesting information to transmit.

You will notice that the string of consecutive "1" 's which the MPU is waiting for is defined as either 10 or 11. This depends on the configuration of the RS-232 setup; if we are set to, say, 1 stop bit, eight data bits, no parity, and one stop bit, then the total *frame length* is 10 – so the MPU will wait for 10 consecutive "1" 's. However, if we are set to, for instance, 1 stop bit, eight data bits, even parity, and on stop bit, then our total frame length is 11 – the MPU will now wait for 11 consecutive "1" 's before waking up.

Bit 1. Transmit Enable (TE)

Setting this bit enables us to transmit data; clearing the bit inhibits this.

Bit 2. Transmit Interrupt Enable (TIE)

A full explanation of this bit requires some knowledge of microprocessor functioning; in particular, the subject of *interrupts*. Whilst not wishing to give a full explanation of the subject in this chapter, a little said on the matter may be helpful.

A microprocessor normally churns away under its own steam, executing code as it goes along. To get a piece of code executed, you normally have to set the start address of the relevant code in the MPU's *program counter* register, perhaps by a jump or branch instruction. However, you may wish to set up a system whereby you have a very important piece of work to be done every so often – perhaps the timing is critical, and this code must be executed, say, once every few milliseconds. Now, in normal operation, you would have to wait for the microprocessor to get round to doing your piece of work – this might be too long. However, with interrupts, you can actually *stop* the MPU from doing what it is, then GO IMMEDIATELY to do a piece of work for you, and then *return* to its original task in the place it left off. As an example, consider the problem of "polling" the keyboard – going to see if any key has been pressed. You may wish to poll the keyboard directly in a loop in software, but this would tie up all the MPU's time, and it would not be able to do any other processing. On the other hand, you may allow the MPU to go and execute some other code; now you may have the problem of the keyboard *never* being polled, or at least very occasionally. You would not want a wait of several seconds in between pressing a key, and the character appearing on the screen!

With interrupts, you will be able to set up a system, linked in to an internal clock, for instance, to poll the keyboard every so often, at a predetermined rate; perhaps every 50 milliseconds.

You will find the enabling of interrupts to be useful in our consideration of communications. The subject will be returned to later.

Bit 3. Receive Enable. (RE)

As with Transmit Enable, TE, above, setting this bit will enable the MPU to receive bits of data. When cleared, nothing will be sent from the MPU.

Bit 4. Receive Interrupt Enable. (RIE)

Again, as with Transmit Interrupt Enable, setting this bit to 1 enables receive interrupts; clearing this bit disables them.

Interrupts on receive may be particularly useful in some circumstances. Consider a terminal, which is both transmitting and receiving characters. Now, transmitting is straightforward – every time a key is pressed, the program transmits that character down the RS-232. Note that this is one case already when we may require interrupts – to poll the keyboard! But, let us instead consider what will be happening on the receive side of things. We will certainly be receiving characters from the host computer. Since we do not know when to expect them, we will have to go to check periodically if anything has been received. But what if we are in the middle of looking at the keyboard when a character is received? If we take too long over polling the keyboard, and *another* character is sent down the line to us, we may miss that one too; indeed, since our first received character will not yet have been cleared form the RECEIVE DATA REGISTER (RDR) mentioned earlier, we will lose both characters and a fatal error will occur.

We may thus find it preferable to *enable receive interrupts*. Thus, every time a character is received, an interrupt will occur, and we will be diverted from our current task to deal with the problem of picking up the received character before it is too late.

In reality, the actual mechanics of interrupts may be rather more complex, and microprocessor-dependent, but the general principle will remain the same.

Bit 5. Transmit Data Register Empty (TDRE)

Consider our process of transmitting characters, one by one. We will pick up a byte of data, corresponding to the character to be sent, and place it in the *transmit data register*. The MPU will now deal with transmitting this character – the mechanics of this will be explained later. However, we will want to know when the Transmit Data Register is ready for the next character – i.e. when it has been emptied.

The TDRE will be set to 1 when this is so; thus, we can periodically check this bit, waiting for it to change to 1. Of course, as soon as we fill up the TDR with another byte of data, TDRE will be reset to 0.

Bit 6. Overrun Framing Error (ORFE)

Basically, this bit will be set to 1 when there has been some sort of receive error. In our example above, dealing with receiving characters, we had the case of one character not having been cleared from the Receive Data Register when another one was subsequently received. In this case we would have had an *overrun error*.

Framing errors occur when the stop bit is 0 – remember that it should always be 1. This means that some error occurred in transmitting or receiving – a bit may have been lost along the way, for instance, or the receiving device may have lost synchronization with the incoming bits.

Bit 7. Receive Data Register Full. (RDRF)

As its name implies, this bit will show us when a whole character has been received, and is available to be picked up (thus clearing the way for the next character).

Rate Mode Control Register

We will now consider the RATE and MODE CONTROL REGISTER (RMCR). This, as its name implies, goes some way towards controlling the *baud rate*, and the *data format*, amongst other things.

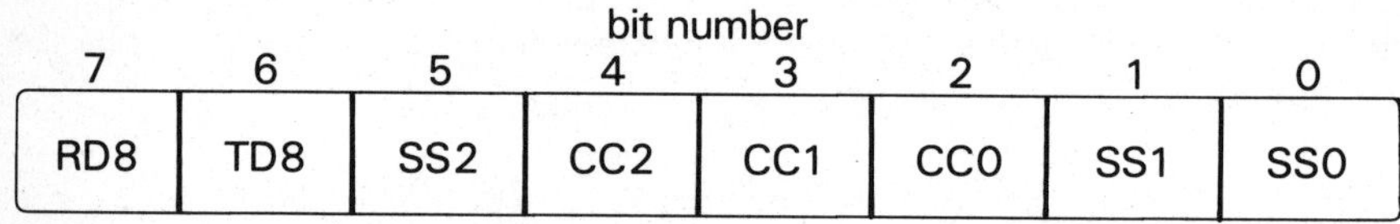

Fig. 7.6 RMCR

Three of the bits (bit 0, bit 1, and bit 5, go some way towards determining the baud rate to be used. Whilst detailed reference to the manufacturer's manuals is really necessary for a full explanation, some guidance will be given here.

The baud rate will be dependent, to a certain extent, on the frequency of the driving clock being used. Different microprocessors usually use different frequency clocks — the clock signal is provided by a crystal oscillator of extremely high frequency. You may have seen reference to "a 4MHz Z80 chip", or "an 8086 running at 6MHz" etc.

Now, the 6303, as with the rest of the family of chips, can run with a number of different crystal frequencies. For instance, we may use a 2.4576 MHz crystal, or a 4.0 MHz one, or a 4.9152 one instead. But the crystal will normally be *divided down by a factor of 4*; thus our effective frequencies to the MPU will be: 614.4 kHz, 1.0 MHz, and 1.2288 MHz.

Suppose we are using a crystal of frequency 2.4576 MHz. Then setting

$SS0=0$; $SS1=0$; and $SS2=0$

would result in the *effective* frequency (that is, the true frequency divided by 4), being further divided by a factor of 16. The end result would be a baud rate of 38400. On the other hand, setting

SS0=1; SS1=0; and SS2=0

would result in the effective frequency being further divided by a factor of 128 – resulting this time in a baud rate of 4800.

The above is for an *asynchronous mode*, which is what we will require for RS-232. We may also wish to use a *clocked synchronous mode*; in this case, for instance, using a 4.0 MHz crystal (which is subsequently divided by 4 to give an effective frequency of 1.0 MHz), and setting

SS0=1; SS1=0; and SS2=0

results in the effective frequency this time being divided by a factor of 16 – the end result is a bit rate of 16 microseconds per bit.

Now, it is only by using SS0 and SS1 that we can alter the baud rate by this method. You will see that there are thus only four possible combinations, i.e.

SS0=0; SS1=0
SS0=1; SS1=0
SS0=0; SS1=1
SS0=1; SS1=1

This will not give us a very wide range of baud rates to choose from!

Instead, the route we shall take is to set SS2=1 (the values of SS0 and SS1 now no longer matter); this means that a separate timer, TIMER 2, will be used to provide the baud rate. You will see later that this means a very wide range of baud rates can be catered for.

We now come to three more bits of the RMCR: bits 2, 3 and 4. These are used to determine the data format and clock source. Again, reference to the manufacturer's manuals is necessary for a full explanation, but we will give examples here.

Setting or clearing these bits will result in different configurations. You will notice that we have 2*2*2, or 8, different combinations of three bits. Different combinations will allow for choices between:

Clocked Synchronous or Asynchronous mode,

8-bit data or 9-bit data,

an External or Internal clock source

and will also determine a particular hardware consideration – whether a particular bit of a particular port is used for input, output, or is unused.

For instance, setting

CC0=1; CC1=0; and CC2=0

results in the following configuration:

8-bit data, asynchronous mode, internal clock source

whilst setting

CC0=1; CC1=0; and CC2=1

will result in:

9-bit data, asynchronous mode, internal clock source.

Finally, you may recall that it is possible to have a configuration in RS-232 such as

1 start bit, 8 data bits, 1 parity bit, and one stop bit.

In this case, our transmit or receive byte (eight bits) is already taken up with the eight bits of data – what will happen with our ninth bit?

The MPU caters for this situation with two spare bits – one for the possible ninth transmit bit, the other for the possible receive bit. These are bits 6 and 7 of the RMCR – bit 6 is the ninth transmit bit, and bit 7 the ninth receive bit, if required.

At the start of this chapter we mentioned a number of other registers, apart from the Transmit and Receive Control Status Register, and the Rate and Mode Control Register. These were:

the Receive Data Register (RDR)

the Receive Data Shift Register (RDSR)

the Transmit Data Register (TDR) and

the Transmit Data Shift Register (TDSR).

Some mention has been made already of the use of these registers above. Let us consider them now in slightly more detail.

The Receive Data and Receive Data Shift Registers

Consider what happens when our MPU is receiving a character. There will be one wire from the outside world, our receive signal line, along which bits of data will be received. The first bit to come in will be a start bit – this will signify the start of a character to be received; it will then be discarded. Suppose we are set to eight bit data, no parity. Then the next bit to be received will be the *least significant bit* of the character, i.e. bit 0. This we take in, and place into the position of BIT 7 of our Receive Data Shift Register. the next bit to be received will be bit 1 of the transmitted character. The process is now *to shift the contents of the receive data shift register one place to the right*, and place the newly-received bit into bit 7 of the RDSR as before.

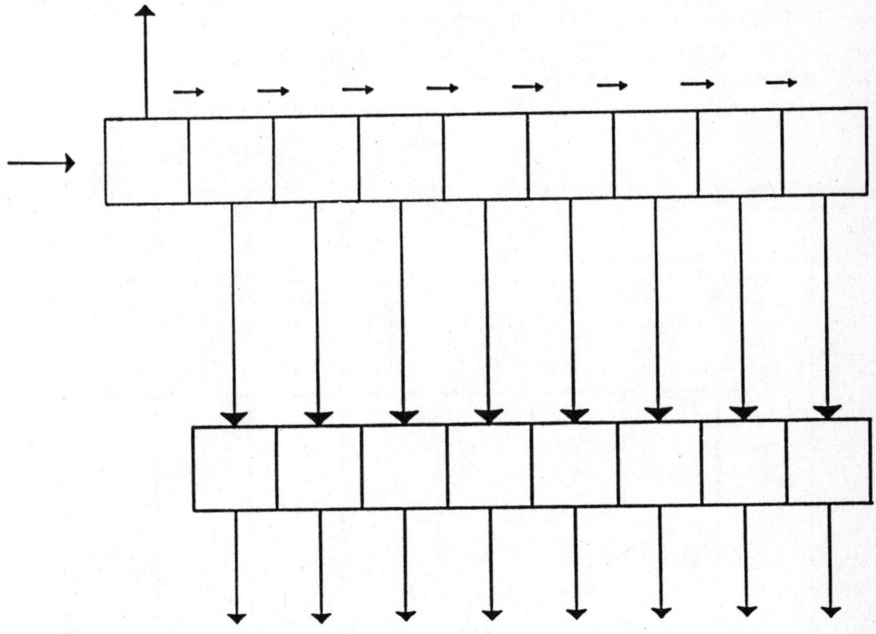

Fig. 7.7 The Receive Registers

This process is continued until all 8 bits have been received. You will now see that our complete 8 bits of data are in the RDSR, the correct way round! The MPU now transfers the whole contents of the RDSR, in parallel, to the Receive Data

Register for us to pick up, and thus frees the RDSR for the next character. This obviously speeds data transfer up considerably)if we can keep up with it), for the current character can be being received into the shift register whilst the previous character is being taken from the data register.

The Transmit Data Shift and Transmit Data Registers.

The transmit registers function in an analogous way to the receive ones. We place a byte of data to be transmitted into the Transmit Data Register. Then, when the Transmit Data Shift Register is empty, the MPU transfers the whole contents of the TDR into the TDSR, and signals that the TDR is empty (by setting the TDRE bit of the TRCSR, you may remember). What does the MPU do now? It transmits the contents of the shift register bit by bit. Of course it first sends a start bit, to signify that a character is on its way. It then *shifts the TDSR one place to the right* – the bit which "falls off" the end is then transmitted. The process is repeated, until all eight bits have been transmitted. You will notice that this procedure automatically means that the least significant bit (bit 0) is transmitted first, then the next least, and so on up to the most significant bit (bit 7).

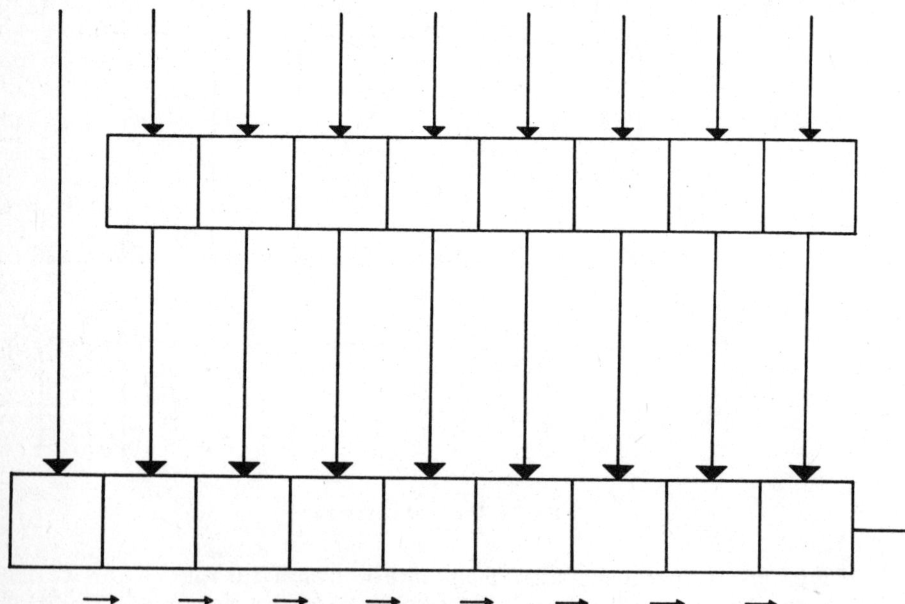

Fig. 7.8 The Transmit Registers

78

Timer 2

We have thus considered all the registers, and all the constituent bits, of the Serial Communications Interface. Before we are able to piece all the bits together into a complete picture, we still have to look at the source of timing. You will remember that, by setting SS0, SS1 and SS2 of the RMCR, we can decide whether the baud rate is predetermined, or can be further determined by the use of TIMER 2 of the MPU.

Timer 2 is an 8-bit reloadable timer, with an output; it is also capable of counting an external event.

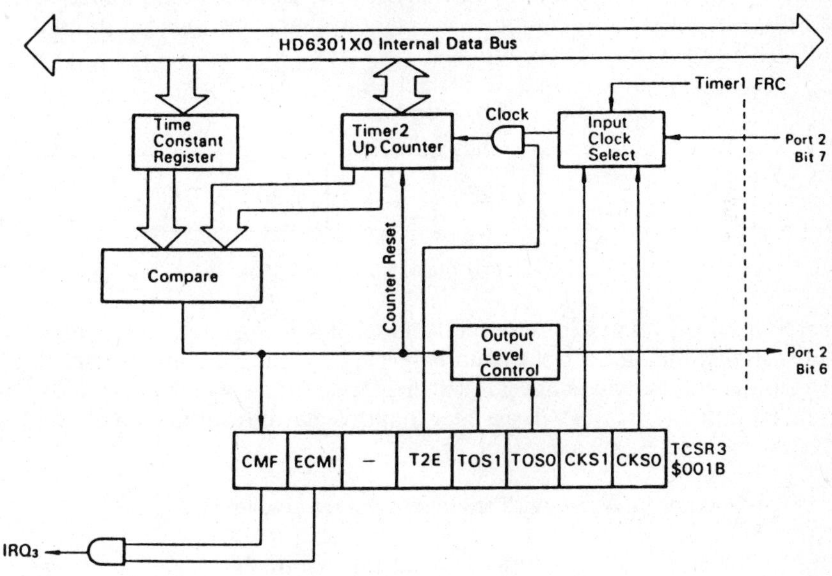

Fig. 7.9 Timer 2 Block Diagram

We have more registers to look at now; timer 2 requires three:

Timer Control Status Register 3 (TCSR3)

Timer 2 Up Counter (T2CNT) and

Timer Constant Register (TCONR).

The way that the timer works is very simple. The up counter, T2CNT, counts up at a given rate (specified, as you will see later, by values in the Timer Control Status Register 3); there will be a constant value in TCONR. When the variable value in T2CNT has reached the value of the constant in TCONR, an output will be triggered. This will, in our case. subsequently go on to provide a steady rate at which to transmit bits of information – the baud rate.

When this match has occurred, the up counter T2CNT is reset to zero, and the counting up starts all over again. Thus a precisely regular series of outputs can be provided for.

Timer Control Status Register 3

As with the registers we have encountered previously, this control register has a number of bits which can be set or cleared depending on the situation. However, it does in fact use only seven out of the eight available bits; bit 5 is unused.

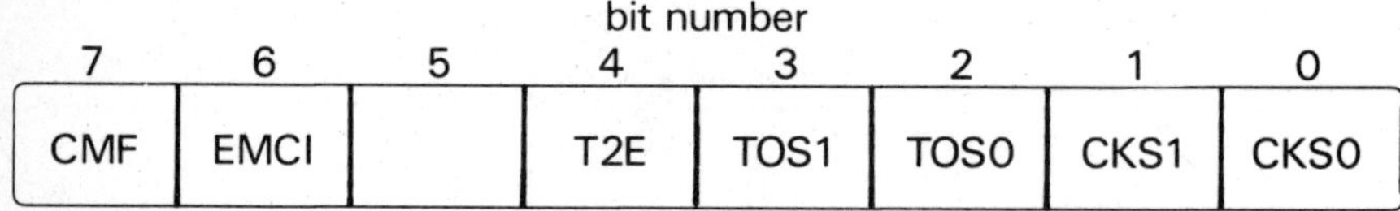

Fig. 7.10 TCSR3

The first two bits, Input Clock Select 0 and Input Clock Select 1, determine the nature of the input clock to the counter. We may wish to use an external clock source under some circumstances; or we may wish to "slow down" the clock, by dividing it by a factor. You will see later that this may be useful in providing for very slow baud rates, such as 50 or 75.

The possible combinations, with their results, are given below:

CKS0	CKS1	Input Clock to the Counter
0	0	E clock
0	1	E clock/8
1	0	E clock/16
1	1	External Clock

Fig. 7.11 CKS0 and CKS1 combinations

E is the *effective clock frequency*, as detailed earlier (remember we will probably be dividing down our actual crystal frequency by a factor of 4).

The next two bits are Timer Output Select 0 (TOS0), and Timer Output Select 1 (TOS1). These, as their names imply, determine the nature of possible timer outputs. Now, for the purposes of setting up this RS-232 system, we are using Timer 2 as the clock source. Thus, we do not require any separate timer output – setting TOS0 and TOS1 both to 0 will inhibit any other timer output. Of course, for other applications we may require a separate 0 or 1 bit to appear at an output location – for some specialist form of communications, for instance. Setting or clearing these bits allows us to specify what the output should be, i.e. always a 1, or always a 0, or whether the output should "toggle" between successive 0's and 1's.

Bit 4 is the Timer 2 Enable Bit (T2E). When this bit is set to 1, clock input to the up counter T2CNT is enable; thus the counter will continue counting up (until it matches the value in the constant register, TCONR). However, clearing this bit will stop the counter.

Bit 5 is not used.

Bit 6 is the Enable Counter Match Interrupt (ECMI). You will no doubt remember *interrupts* from previous discussions on some of the other registers. As you may by now expect, setting this bit enables us to interrupt the MPU in whatever it is doing, everytime a match occurs between the up counter and the constant register. This may be useful, indeed vital, for particular applications; it will not be necessary in our case, since the MPU is already taking good care of our special RS-232 needs.

Bit 7 is the Counter Match Flag (CMF). Quite simply, this bit is set to 1 when a match occurs between the up counter T2CNT and the constant register TCONR.

You may now wonder how Timer 2 is useful for providing baud rates. The system we may use is to place in the constant register TCONR a particular value for a particular baud rate; then, when a match occurs, the MPU will be signalled to output one bit of data; this timing will be regular, and thus we will have generated our required baud rate.

Now, the resultant baud rate can be calculated by the following expression:

Baud Rate = (Input Clock Frequency to Timer 2)/(32*(Value of TCONR + 1))

We can thus calculate the necessary values of TCONR, for any given baud rate, and any given input clock frequency.

For instance, for a crystal of frequency 4.9152 MHz, which gives an effective input clock frequency of 1.2288 MHz, the values for the Timer 2 Constant Register to give various baud rates are:

Baud Rate	TCONR Value
150	255
300	127
600	63
1200	31
2400	15
4800	7
9600	3
19200	1

Fig. 7.12 4.9152 MHz crystal

(Note that a value of 0 would give us a rather improbable baud rate of 38400!).

So, if we require a baud rate of, say, 1200, we place the value of 31 into the Timer 2 Constant Register TCONR, and set the up counter going.

If we are using a crystal of a different frequency, then the above values for the TCONR will be different. This is where the choice of crystal may be significant. For instance, consider a 4.0 MHz crystal:

Baud Rate	TCONR Value
150	207
300	101
600	51
1200	25
2400	12

Fig. 7.13 4.0 MHz crystal

We would thus not be able to generate a baud rate of higher than 2400, which may be too restricting.

We now have available all the necessary tools to construct our software for the communications system. Since the software has to operate at a very low level (i.e. it operates directly on registers of the MicroProcessor Unit), and since it also has to operate very quickly (for there may be quite a lot going on to keep up with a high baud rate), we shall develop the software in *assembly language*.

The Hitachi 6303 microprocessor Central Processing Unit (CPU) we are considering has two internal 8-bit registers for its own use

– the *accumulators* – labelled the A and B registers. These may, in some case, be lumped together to make up one, 16-bit, register, called the D register. There is also one other 16-bit register, called the X register, and an 8-bit register which contains FLAGS – bits which are set to 0 or 1 depending on the results of previously executed instructions.

Consider the steps we have to take to provide RS-232 communications. We first have to *set up* all of the MPU registers; we will have to configure them for data format, baud rate, clock rate etc. Then having done this, we can safely go into our *communications mode*, both transmitting and receiving bytes of data.

The SETUP

In fact, before we do any setting up at all, it will be advisable to RESET the Transmit/Receive Control Status Register, so that we start from a known, given state:

```
LDAA        #20H
STAA        TRCSR
```

We thus load the A accumulator with the value 20 hexadecimal; that is, 32 decimal or 0010 0000 in binary. You will see the effect this has on the TRCSR:

Receive Data Register Full (RDRF) is reset to 0 – indicating that the register is in fact empty.

OverRun Framing Error register (ORFE) is reset to 0 – indicating that here is no overrun or framing error.

Transmit Data Register Empty is set to 1 – indicating that the TDR is in fact empty.

Receive Interrupt Enable (RIE) is reset to 0; we do not here require receive interrupts to be running.

Receive Enable (RE) is reset to 0, as we are not yet ready to receive anything.

Transmit Interrupt Enable (TIE) is also reset to 0; we do not require transmit interrupts either.

Wake Up (WU) is, finally, reset to 0; we will not be requiring this feature.

We can now set the Rate and Mode Control Register (RMCR). Suppose we require the following configuration:

8-bit data, asynchronous, using Timer 2 as the internal clock

Reference to the manuals will show that we thus require:

$SS0=0$; $SS1=0$; and $SS2=1$,

for you may recall that setting SS2 to 1 means that it is Timer 2 that provides the clock input for the Serial Communications Interface.

We also require:

$CC0=1$; $CC1=0$; and $CC2=0$,

to specify that we want 8-bit, asynchronous data.

Since we are specifying 8-bit data, and do not require a ninth bit, we can reset Transmit Data bit 8 (TD) and Receive Data bit 8 (RD8) to 0, and leave them so.

You will thus see that we need to SET bits 2 and 4, and leave the rest at 0. i.e. our register requires the bit-pattern:

0010 0100 in binary, or 24 in hexadecimal.

So to set up the RMCR, we have to:

```
LDAA        #24H
STAA        RMCR
```

So we have now set up our data format; but what about the baud rate? This is provided for by Timer 2 – we can now set up the constant register according to our required baud rate.

Suppose we are using a crystal of frequency 4.9152 MHz, and require a baud rate of 9600. Then we need to put the value of 3 into the Timer 2 Constant Register (TCONR):

```
LDAA        #3
STAA        TCONR
```

We can now set up the Timer 2 Control Status Register 3 (TCSR3). Referring to the description of this register above, you will see that we need to do the following:

set CKS0 (Input Clock Select 0) and CKS1 (Input Clock Select 1) to 0; we are not dividing down the input clock any further

set TOS0 (Timer 2 Output Select 0) and TOS1 (Timer 2 Output Select 1) to 0, as we do not require any timer 2 output, other than that provided by the Serial Communications Interface already we do not require any interrupts from a match of the counter – thus Enable Counter Match Flag (ECMI – bit 6) is reset to 0

we DO require to enable the Timer 2; this is done by setting the Timer 2 Enable flag (T2E – bit 4) to 1

finally, the Counter Match Flag (CMF – bit 7) is READ ONLY anyway. This means that, whilst we can certainly go to look at its current value, we are not able to make any change to that ourselves.

Thus, to set up the TCSR3, we

```
LDAA         #10H
STAA         TCSR3
```

for 10 hexadecimal is 0001 0000 in binary; we thus set bit 4 only, and clear the rest.

We next have to set up the Transmit/Receive Control Status Register (TRCSR), which we have, you will remember, previously reset. But, before we do this, attention will have to be paid to a requirement of the MPU. For, when clearing the Transmit Enable (TE) and Receive Enable (RE) bits of the TRCSR, and then setting them again (to ENABLE transmit and receive), it is necessary to allow for a delay of more than *one bit cycle of the current baud rate*. For if we set TE and/or RE in less than this time, the internal transmit and receive initialization may fail.

We thus include a (baud-dependent) delay loop, for instance:

```
        LDX #DELAY_VALUE
LOOP:   DEX
        BNE LOOP
```

where the delay value is chosen to provide the correct length of delay, for a given baud rate (and a given execution rate of the loop, which will depend on the crystal frequency).

We can now, finally, set up the Transmit and Receive Control Status Register. What do we require? Reference to the above description of this register will show that we need to do a number of things:

Enable the Transmit and Receive functions

Disable any interrupts (we are not using these)

Disable Wake Up

Clear any error flag

Indicate that the Receive Data Register is EMPTY

Indicate that the Transmit Data Register is EMPTY

We thus need to:

SET bits 1 and 3 (TE and RE) and

CLEAR all of the other bits.

So the required bit pattern is:

0010 1010 in binary, or 2A in hexadecimal.

Thus the instructions we require to set up the TRCSR are:

```
LDAA        #2A
STAA        TRCSR
```

We now need to note another important point about the functioning of the Serial Communications Interface. The manufacturers state that, during the start-up procedure, when the Rate and Mode Control Register and the Transmit and Receive Control Register have been set up, and when the Transmit Enable (TE) bit of the TRCSR has been set, then the SCI will produce a 10-bit (or 11-bit, depending on the data format chosen) *preamble of bits*; when the preamble is produced, it has the effect of stabilizing the internal synchronization of the SCI. After this preamble has been produced, the transmitter is ready to act.

We thus have to first wait for this preamble of data bits to be produced, before we are able to go ahead and use the SCI. A convenient way of doing this is to wait for the transmit buffer to empty. You may remember from the description of the Transmit and Receive Control Status Register that bit 5 is the Transmit Data Register Empty flag; the bit is 0 if the data register is full, but is set to 1 when it becomes empty. Thus all we have to do is to continually poll this bit, waiting for it to change from 0 to 1. This can be accomplished by a *bit test*:

```
LOOP1:          BTST5,TRCSR
                BEQ         LOOP1
```

Finally, we clear up any mess left in two of the registers after this start-up procedure – the Transmit and Receive Control Status Register and the Receive Data Register. The manufacturers of the chip state:

"When a few bits are set between bit 5 to bit 7 in the TRCSR, a read of the TRCSR is sufficient for clearing those bits. It is not necessary to read the TRCSR everytime to clear each bit".

We can thus just perform a read of the TRCSR to clear up any bits which may have been set during the internal synchronization period – for instance, the Over Run and Framing Error bit – and also read the RDR to empty it of any unwanted data left in there.

```
LDAA        TRCSR
LDAA        RDR
```

Communications Mode

We have thus performed the set-up operation, to get the Serial Communications Interface already for use; so we can now get down to the real business of communications – transmitting and receiving characters, and hence files.

First of all, we must learn to walk before we can run. Let us consider the two primitives of:

i) how to transmit a single character
ii) how to receive a single character

Both of these will, in fact, turn out to be very easy, because the SCI will do almost all of the work for us.

Let us look at how to transmit a character. Suppose the character is at some address in memory, say at char__start. Then we first pick up the character

```
LDX         #CHAR_START
LDAA        0,X
```

You will see later that this procedure can be expanded into dealing with a whole string of characters, i.e. a file. With this end in mind, there may be two things now to consider. First, we will have to deal with whatever handshaking is going on, and second, this may not be the first character that has been transmitted – we may be in the middle of a string of characters.

We can actually cater for the handshaking now, but deal with it in practice later, by putting a jump to a subroutine for the handshaking code. This jump will return to just after the calling point at the end of execution, so that we can then carry on with the matter in hand. Our next line of code will thus be:

```
JSR         HAND_SHAKE
```

That is the first point dealt with. Now for the second. You may well remember the functioning of the SCI in transmitting a character – we place the byte of data to be transmitted into the TRANSMIT DATA REGISTER, and then when the

TRANSMIT DATA SHIFT REGISTER is clear, the SCI will pick up this new byte, put it into the TDSR, and subsequently transmit it. Now, we obviously will have to wait until the Transmit Data Register is empty, before putting in our new byte (if we are not to overwrite old data before it is transmitted); but there is an easy way for us to check this. You will remember that bit 5 of the Transmit and Receive Control Status Register (TRCSR) is used for indicating whether the TDR is full or empty—it is set to 1 if empty, and 0 if full. We can thus *poll* this bit, waiting for it to indicate that the register is empty (you may also remember this procedure from our set up procedure):

```
LOOP2:          BTST          5,TRCSR
                BEQ             LOOP2
```

When the register becomes empty, the program will fall out of the loop, and on to the next line. We are now free to place the new byte of data (held still in the A register) into the Transmit Data Register:

```
STAA          TDR
```

And that is all there is to it—the Serial Communications Interface takes care of the rest!

How about receiving a character? Again, the SCI will do most of the work for us, for it will automatically read the byte of received data bit by bit into the Receive Data Shift Register, and then transfer the contents, when all is received, into the Receive Data Register (RDR). We can then pick up this new byte of data. There are now three items that must be considered. As with transmitting, there will probably be handshaking to cater for. We may also be in the middle of a string of characters which are being received into a file. Additionally, there may have been an error in receiving the character, so this will have to be checked.

First, let's find somewhere to put the character once received. Suppose the address of this location in memory is REC_CHAR. We then load the X register with this address, ready for later on:

```
LDX          #REC_CHAR
```

We now have to cater for the handshaking. As before, we can for the moment just put in jumps to the relevant pieces of code, which will be dealt with later. In fact, we will require *two* separate handshake routines—remember that WE are now controlling what is going on, so we have to be able to tell the transmitting device *when to start* and *when to stop*. These two routines will be called, say, START_HAND and STOP_HAND.

So, first of all, we signal to the transmitting device that it is all right to start transmitting:

```
JSR         START_HAND
```

This done, we can wait and receive any character which is subsequently transmitted. In a similar manner to the case of transmitting a byte, there is a flag in the Transmit and Receive Control Status Register which is used to indicate when the Receive Data Register is full, i.e. when a new byte of data has been received. This is bit 7. We thus simply have to continually poll this bit, waiting for it to indicate that it is full. The bit, you may recall, is set to 0 when the register is empty, and 1 when it is full:

```
LOOP3:      BTST        7,TRCSR         ; bit test
    BEQ         LOOP3               ; branch if equal to 0
```

When the register is full, we can pick it up:

```
LDAA        RDR
```

Now comes an extra consideration – was there any error in reception? There is yet another bit of the TRCSR which we can check for this – the Over Run and Framing Error bit (ORFE, which is bit 6). This will be clear if there is no error:

```
BTST 6,TRCSR
BNE ERROR     ; branch if not equal to error routine
```

For an error handling routine, we might wish to set some error flag, to indicate later that an error message should be displayed, and perhaps clear the byte of received data (since we know it is rubbish):

```
ERROR:      LDAA            #FFH
    STAA            ERROR_FLAG      ; set flag to 255 decimal

    CLRA                            ; this register returned
                                    ; with RDR value
```

However, if the byte of data has been received correctly, we can save it in the designated area:

```
STAA        0,X                 ; X is address of area
                                ; to save byte
```

We may now, finally, want to indicate to the transmitting machine that it should not send any more characters; this will be dealt with by our STOP__HAND routine:

```
JSR         STOP_HAND           ; jump to subroutine
```

Handshaking Routines

You will remember that our communications package will probably offer the user a choice of handshaking protocols. In our case, the choice will probably be between NONE, RTS/CTS, and XON/XOFF. NONE is easy! But we will obviously have to cater for the choice of either RTS/CTS (hardware handshaking) and XON/XOFF (software handshaking).

First of all, we will deal with the *transmit* handshaking routine – HAND __SHAKE. There will be two entry points, one for hardware handshaking and the other for software. We will in reality need some system of knowing which handshaking system is being used – a flag for instance. However, that lies in the functioning of the communications package as a whole; we will here consider just the handshaking features, first for hardware handshaking.

The protocol for hardware handshaking is as follows. Suppose that we are the transmitting device, assigned as the Data Communications Equipment (DCE). Then, the receiving device will be Data Terminal Equipment (DTE); it will be controlling the Request To Send signal line (RTS). This will be HIGH (logic 1) when the DTE is not ready to receive, and LOW (logic 0) otherwise. Now, the RTS line will be tied in to some *port* of the Micro Processor Unit – in the case of the 6303X under consideration, this may be one of the bits of PORT2, for example. We can thus poll this bit, which will be set to 1 or 0 depending on the state of the RTS line (if the hardware is working correctly!); if it is set to 1 we will have to wait for it to change to 0 before we are able to transmit a character:

```
RTSCTS:                        ; entry point for RTS/CTS
   BTST        RTS,PORT2       ; RTS is relevant bit
number
   BNE         RTSCTS


   RTS                         ; return from subroutine
```

XON/XOFF Handshaking

Suppose we now consider the software handshaking option, and in particular XON/XOFF. (There are other types of software handshaking, one of which will be considered later). The way this works is simple. Two *control codes* are used – Device Control 1 (DC1) and Device Control 3 (DC3), for XON and XOFF respectively. If the receiving device sends US an XOFF, it means that we must *stop transmitting*. If, on the other hand, it sends us an XON, then it means that we can start transmitting again. So, before we transmit a character, we must check to see if any character has been received. If not, it is safe to transmit the character. However, if an XOFF has been received, we must patiently wait for the receiving device to send us an XON:

```
XONXOFF:                  ; entry point for XON/XOFF
        BTST  7,TRCSR     ; anything received?
        BEQ END           ; return if nothing

        LDAA  RDR         ; data from receive reg.
        CMPA  #13H         ; is it a DC3 (XOFF)?
        BNE END           ; return if not
LOOP4:                    ; now wait for XON
        BTST  7,TRCSR     ; wait for character
        BEQ   LOOP4       ; .. if nothing received
        LDAA  RDR         ; when something is rec'd
        CMPA  #11H         ; is it an XON?
        BNE   LOOP4       ; go back if not

END:
        RTS
```

That deals with handshaking routines for transmitting. Now let us consider what is required when we are receiving.

Handshaking Routines for Receiving

You will remember that we have two cases here: we may wish to either indicate that we *are not* ready to receive anything, or indicate that we *are* ready to receive. Again, both of these cases must in turn be split into two; for we may be using either hardware handshaking (in this case, RTS/CTS), or software handshaking (e.g. XON/XOFF). First consider *hardware handshaking*. Our routine for indicating that we are ready to receive is START_HAND:

```
START_HAND:              ; entry point for handshaking
```

Remember that we are the Data Communications Equipment (DCE) – our signal line for handshaking is the Clear To Send (CTS). Its functioning is quite simple. All we have to do is to set it HIGH)logic 1) when we are not ready to receive, and LOW (logic 0) when we are ready to receive. As with the RTS line, our CTS signal line will be mapped into a port location of the MPU again, perhaps PORT 2 as before. So, since we are ready to receive, we clear this port location bit; the hardware of the RS-232 interface will then set the CTS signal line to 0:

```
BCLR CTS,PORT2    ; bit clear
```

Suppose, on the other hand, that we are using XON/XOFF handshaking. Then, in this case, all we have to do is to send an XON control code (DC1) to indicate that we are ready to receive data. We have already, fortunately, constructed a routine to transmit one byte of data, called TRANSMIT. This transmitted the contents of the A register. So all we have to do is:

```
        LDAA #11H              ; XON control code
        JSR TRANSMIT
```

The two complementary routines for STOP__HAND are just as
straightforward. IF we are using hardware handshaking, we simply set the CTS
line HIGH to disable data input:

```
        STOP_HAND:
             BSET CTS,PORT2
```

whilst for the case of XON/XOFF handshaking, we send an XOFF control
code (i.e. DC3):

```
             LDAA Î3H
             JSR TRANSMIT
```

File Transfer Routines

These simple subroutines can be built up quite easily into routines to transfer
whole lines, and hence whole files, of data. For suppose we wish to send a string
of characters, which start at the address CHAR__START. We will need to know
either how many characters we are to transmit, or we can send a *record delimiter*.
Suppose we do the latter, and we use as a delimiter a CARRIAGE RETURN
control code (CR, which is 0D in hexadecimal, or 13 in decimal).

```
        SEND_LINE:
             LDX #CHAR_START
             INX               ; increment address
                               ; to point at next
                               ; character
             LDAA 0.X          ; pick up character
             JSR TRANSMIT      ; and transmit it
             CMPA #0DH         ; is it end of line?
             BNE SEND_LINE     ; if not, go back for
                               ; another one

             RTS               ; the end
```

Conversely, we may wish to receive a string of characters (terminated by a
Carriage Return), and save them in memory.

```
        RECEIVE_LINE:
             LDX #REC_CHAR     ; start address of
                               ; where to save
                               ; characters
             JSR START_HAND    ; o.k. to receive
        RECA:
```

```
        JSR RECEIVE        ; rec've a char.
        STAA 0,X           ; save character
        INX                ; ready for next
                           ; character
        CMPA #0DH          ; is it a CR?
         BNE RECA          ; back for more
                           ; if not
        RTS                ; .. otherwise,
                           ; the end
```

Finer points of Detail on Assembler Language Coding

Those of you with some experience in developing software in an assembler language will notice some points of detail about the preceding examples, which are glossed over as there is no wish to confuse the reader unnecessarily. For instance, different assemblers will use different standards for mnemonics. The above standard used is that specified by Hitachi; however, altenative assemblers may accept

```
    LDA A,#0
```

instead of

```
    LDAA #0
```

for instance.

Also, all of the unresolved addresses will have to be resolved at some time. For instance, we might include a file which contains a list of EQU's, as follows:

```
    RTS      EQU      4
    CTS      EQU      5
    PORT2    EQU      3
    RMCR     EQU     10H
    TRCSR    EQU     11H
    RDR      EQU     12H
    TDR      EQU     13H
```

and so forth, for any unresolved addresses.

Finally, there is a great variety of ways to express numbers in hexadecimal. You may see, amongst others:

```
    10H,    &10, or $10.
```

CHAPTER 8

Communication Via The Telephone Network

With all our knowledge of how communications works in principle, and in practice, we can now advance on to perhaps the most exciting part of communications – making computers talk over telephone networks. This is not a new subject; indeed, many large corporations have, for a decade or more, been using large scale communications to enable mainframe computers to talk to each other, or to have terminals connected to a computer many miles away. Consider a company like British Aerospace, for instance. Part of its Aircraft Division comprises the sites at Weybridge, in Surrey, and Filton, Bristol. However, the mainframe used is at the Weybridge site – Filton users communicate with the Weybridge computer via a number of dedicated telephone lines.

However, communications over telephone lines has only recently become popular, and accessible, for the small business, and indeed the home hobbyist. This has been partly fuelled by its tremendous popularity in the U.S.A.– due to no small degree to the cheapness (local calls being free) of the telephone network, compared to U.K. and European standards. The public's awareness has also been heightened by the numerous press and television reports of "hackers" breaking into supposedly secure databases via the telephone lines – often with mischievous results!

But how is this feat of communications to be accomplished? The answer lies, for the microcomputer market at least, with (yet again) the RS-232.

8.1 Talking to the Outside World

You will have realized by now that we are happy when communicating over short distances – typically just a few meters – and using an interconnecting cable to transmit and receive the data. All of this can be accomplished quite successfully using one of the communications standards already described; usually still the RS-232-C interface, although others are sometimes popular too. But how are we to do the same sort of thing when using a telephone line? If the distance we had to communicate over using the telephone lines was quite small, you might

95

be tempted to rip out the wires from you telephone socket, and connect one up to the Transmit Data line, one to the Receive Data line, one to the RTS line of the RS-232, and so forth. British Telecom would not be amused!

Another consideration is that, under normal circumstances, we do not have exclusive use of a telephone line when we are making a telephone call. There tend to be a number of voices sharing the line at any one time – perhaps as many as a dozen. This is known as *multiplexing*. Of course, we do not hear all of these other voices as well as our own – everything would be quite unintelligible if this were so. The method used in multiplexing is *time sharing*; telecommunications researchers have found that a voice does not need to be transmitted continuously for satisfactory performance. Instead, you might have, say, five different voices using the same line. But each voice takes it in turn to use the line for a very short time, until it is the next voice's turn to use the line. This cycle continues around, with control going back to the first voice, and so forth.

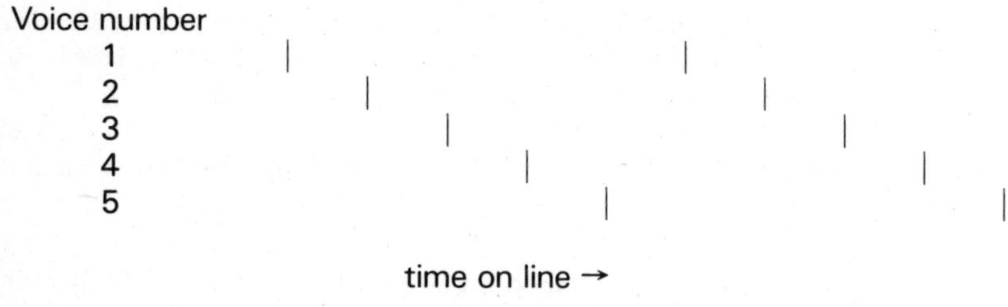

Fig. 8.1 Time Sharing (Multiplexing)

Of course, this happens very quickly, with each turn lasting a minute fraction of a second. But it is all too quick for the human ear to notice. Nevertheless, if we are to use telephone lines for computer communications, then this will have to be taken into account as well.

What is required is some kind of device which will interface between the RS-232 of our computer, and a standard telephone line. It will be able to accept RS-232 input and transmit it over the line. Conversely, any received data will have to be converted into an RS-232 standard before being passed onto us. Many such devices are readily available on the market; we need not worry ourselves with their exact workings; as long as we can successfully connect our RS-232 interface to them, everything else will be taken care of for us!

8.2 Modems and Acoustic Couplers

This, then, is the task of *modems* and *acoustic couplers*. (Modem stands for MOdulator/DEModulator). What is the difference between these two devices?

It is simply that a modem connects directly into the telephone socket, thus bypassing the handset. An acoustic coupler, on the other hand, utilizes the telephone handset – the acoustic coupler has two rubber cups intowhich the handset can be inserted.

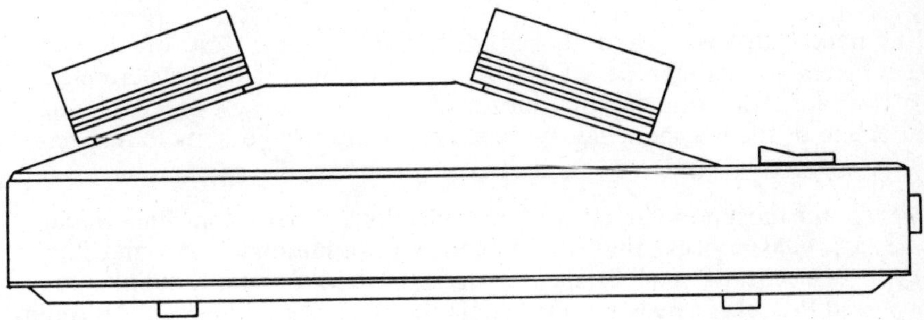

Fig. 8.2 An Acoustic Coupler

So the operation should be (hopefully) fairly straight-forward; we connect a cable between the RS-232 interface of our computer and the RS-232 of the modem or acoustic coupler, and then (in the case of a modem) plug the modem into the telephone socket on the wall. With an acoustic coupler we insert the telephone handset into the rubber cups of the device.

Unfortunately, we will immediately come up against the old problem of wiring up the interface lead. Examples will be given later in this book as an illustration of wiring up interfaces in practice, but not all computers, printers, modems and the like can be covered! At the end of the day, unfortunately, one has to resort to the manufacturer's manual, and the description of pin connections for the interface.

However, later in this chapter we will describe, as an example, one particular make of acoustic coupler, and how to connect to it successfully.

8.3 Baud Rates

In the past we have favoured using the highest speed possible when communicating with the RS-232; this obviously serves to give the quickest data transfer rate. You will probably have guessed by now, if you did not already know from practical experience, that 9600 baud is the favourite speed for most applications. However, remember that the specification for the RS-232 interface stipulates that transmission cables will be less than about 50 feet in length; it is only with the later specification of RS-449/422 that the distance increases considerably. You will thus probably not be surprised to hear that transmission rates when using telephone lines are drastically reduced, even though we are not using direct RS-232 communications. In practice, a baud rate of 1200 is the highest used; indeed, perhaps the most popular is still 300 baud.

The baud rate used, and indeed the choice of the rest of the setup parameters – parity, number of data bits, etc.– will naturally be determined by what we are connecting to. This time the tune is called entirely be what is on the other end of the telephone line; we will have to conform exactly to that setup.

Perhaps the most popular use of communications via telephone lines is that of *electronic mail* services – the use of databases, information services, and literally sending "electronic" mail by such services as Telecom Gold, Easylink, One to One, and Prestel. There is a limited choice of baud rates to be used, depending on which service is dialled into. For example, Telecom Gold has a 300/300 baud line (that is, the transmit speed is 300 baud, and the receive speed is 300 baud), a 1200/1200 baud line, and also a 1200/75 baud line. Why is there a choice?

8.4 Full and Half Duplex

We have, without mentioning the fact, implicitly considered already both *full duplex* and *half duplex* systems. Basically, the end result of the difference between these two systems is that full duplex means that both transmission and reception is going on by both ends at the same time, whereas with half duplex, the transmit and receive functions are kept separate. Thus a terminal works in a full duplex mode, for we can both type in characters on the keyboard (which subsequently appear on the screen), and also receive characters from the host computer. However, a simple file transfer program is clearly one-way, for any characters received by this program will be missed or discarded (except for control characters such as XON and XOFF).

A consequence of this, which you may remember from a previous chapter, is the subject of *local* or *host echo*. A terminal, in full duplex mode, will not place a character input from the keyboard directly onto the screen. Instead, the terminal transmits the character to the host computer, which subsequently *echoes* the character back to the terminal; when this character is received, it is of course displayed on the screen. Now, a half duplex system will not be able to do this. When in transmit mode, any character input and transmitted will also have to be displayed on the screen, since there is no facility for receiving characters (which may have been echoed back).

Thus, systems which use 300/300 baud, or 1200/1200 baud, generally tend to be full duplex; you will need a terminal or terminal emulator to operate them. However, 1200/75 may be a half duplex system.

The fact that there are different systems, maintained for the same service even, is due to a number of reasons. There are many acoustic couplers still on the market with a maximum baud rate of only 300; such equipment tends to be cheaper. Also, many of the "bulletin boards" are run by small concerns, and may use equipment which supports only 300 baud.

As an example, we will describe here one popular acoustic coupler on the market – the Epson CX-21.

8.5 Epson CX-21

The Epson CX-21 acoustic coupler is a small, portable device, typical of many on the market. Connection to the telephone, as mentioned before, is by plugging the mouth and ear pieces of the handset into two rubber cups of the acoustic coupler – making sure that the handset is the right way round! (There is a diagram on the device to ensure that this is done correctly).

There are two switches to allow a choice of operation – the first is Mode Switch 1, which selects operation between either *originate* or *answer* mode. What does this mean?

In a similar way to our having to make the distinction between two devices connected together via the RS-232 (one, you will remember, is labelled DTE, and the other DCE; this determines which one uses which wire for transmit and receive), we will have to decide how to distinguish between our two devices connected together over the telephone line.

There is thus a choice of two modes for each device – Originate or Answer. Obviously Originate and Answer can talk to each other – not so for Originate to Originate or Answer to Answer. It is conventional for the modem on the side which is initiating the call to be in the originate mode, and the modem on the side that is receiving the call to be in the answer mode. Thus, when dialling up a service such as Telecom Gold, one would put the modem or acoustic coupler in to the *originate mode*.

From a practical point of view, it is the answer side which initiates the whistling tone you might hear. This is the carrier frequency tone. Thus, you could, if you wished, dial up one of the available services; all you would hear is this whistling tone.

Mode Switch 2 allows you to choose between *full duplex* and *half duplex* (and there is a test mode as well). Normally, you would be using full duplex.

Another useful feature is a *ready indicator*. This is a light emitting diode (LED) that lights up when a carrier signal is being received – you do not have to listen for it yourself! It indicates that both of the modems on either end of the telephone line are ready. Of course, if the light goes off, you know that there has been a break in the transmission, and the modem set to answer has given up producing a carrier signal.

The RS-232 Connector

There is also the, by now expected, 25-pin D-type connector for the RS-232. This has, inscribed above it, the marking "DTE". Do not be fooled by this! It actually means that it should be connected to DTE – for it is wired as DCE. The pin connections are given below:

<table>
<tr><td>Pin number</td><td>Function</td></tr>
<tr><td>1</td><td>Protective ground</td></tr>
<tr><td>2</td><td>TxD. Data input to the CX-21</td></tr>
<tr><td>3</td><td>RxD. Data output from CX-21</td></tr>
<tr><td>5</td><td>Clear To Send (CTS). Controlled by CX-21
This signal line is set when the carrier is detected – it indicates that transmission is enabled.</td></tr>
<tr><td>6</td><td>Data Set Ready (DSR). Controlled by CX-21.
This signal line is set whenever the power is on – it simply indicates that the modem is on.</td></tr>
<tr><td>7</td><td>Signal ground.</td></tr>
<tr><td>8</td><td>Data Carrier Detect (DCD). Controlled by the CX-21.
It is set when the carrier is being received.</td></tr>
</table>

Fig. 8.3 CX-21 Wiring

You will notice that everything is happily quite standard. There are no input control lines to the CX-21, such as RTS (pin 4) or DTR (pin 20) which we might have to be careful to cater for. The three control lines which the CX-21 enables or disables need not concern us too much – they are all just used to indicate that everything is on and ready to go.

Generally, for electronic mail services and the like, we will be using software handshaking—XON/XOFF. So our interconnecting cable needs only three wires—TXD (pin 2), RXD (pin 3) and Signal Ground (pin 7). Thus if we are connected as DTE, the following wiring will be suitable:

pin numbers

DTE (us)   DCE (CX-21)

2 _________________ 2

3 _________________ 3

7 _________________ 7

Fig. 8.4

However, if the device we are using is wired as DCE, there is no need to panic—we can simply swap pins 2 and 3 over:

pin numbers

DCE (us)   DCE (CX-21)

2 _________________ 3

3 _________________ 2

7 _________________ 7

Fig. 8.5

Given that we have now successfully wired up an interconnecting lead, the next step for us is to configure our terminal, or whatever we are using, to suit the system we are going to "log in" to. For instance, we might be using the 300 baud Telecom Gold service. We would thus need to set up for:

300 baud (transmit and receive)
7 data bits
Even parity
1 stop bit
Xon/Xoff handshaking
Host echo

We would then dial up the required number on the telephone, wait for the whistling tone (which means we are connected through to the computer on the other end), plug the handset into the rubber cups of the acoustic coupler, wait for the Ready light to go on, and then hit a few carriage returns on the keyboard to try to get some response. We should, if all is correct, now see the welcome message from Telecom Gold. We are all set to go!

CHAPTER 9

Parallel Interfacing

9.1 Why Use Parallel?

We have, up until now, been concerned primarily with *serial* interfaces. You may remember from the early part of the book that various types of communications systems were explored in principle. There were seen to be two possibilities. The first was a system which used *one wire* only for transmission (apart from the signal ground, of course). This meant that our byte of data, comprising *eight bits*, had to be transmitted *bit by bit*, i.e. in a bit serial fashion. However, there was also shown to be a second way around this problem. We could use *eight* separate wires, one for each bit, and thus transmit each of the eight bits, and hence a whole byte of data, at the same time. This is known as *bit parallel* transfer.

Serial interfaces, such as the RS-232, are most popular and widely used. They offer distinct advantages in simplicity and ease of use, and not least cheapness of interconnecting wires!

However, parallel interfaces offer distinct advantages too. It is readily seen that that data can be transferred more quickly by a factor of at least eight, since all eight bits of a byte are transmitted at the same time. (Remember, too, that for an asynchronous system like RS-232 two bits – the start bit and stop bit – are effectively wasted).

Parallel interfaces are indeed also as popular, if not more so, than serial interfaces with manufacturers. Almost every piece of computer hardware will have a parallel interface as standard, whilst an RS-232 interface may be regarded as an add-on feature. This is largely due to the fact that printer manufacturers – for a printer is, in general, the most likely piece of equipment to be hooked up to a parallel interface – still largely favour the parallel interface as a standard connector.

There are numerous reasons for this situation. The main reason is that a parallel interface is quite often very cheap to include in the design of a microcomputer. Most of the "home" microcomputers available have the parallel interface, or "printer port", at the back of the machine. It is actually just the rear edge of the printed circuit board, with suitable cutouts, that the plug will fit into.

103

i) Serial transfer

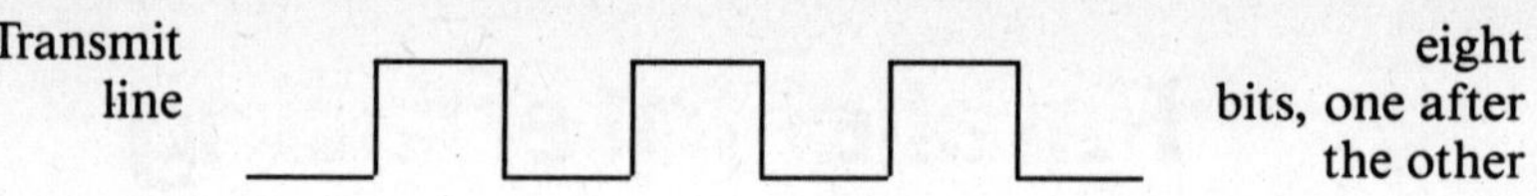

ii) Parallel transfer

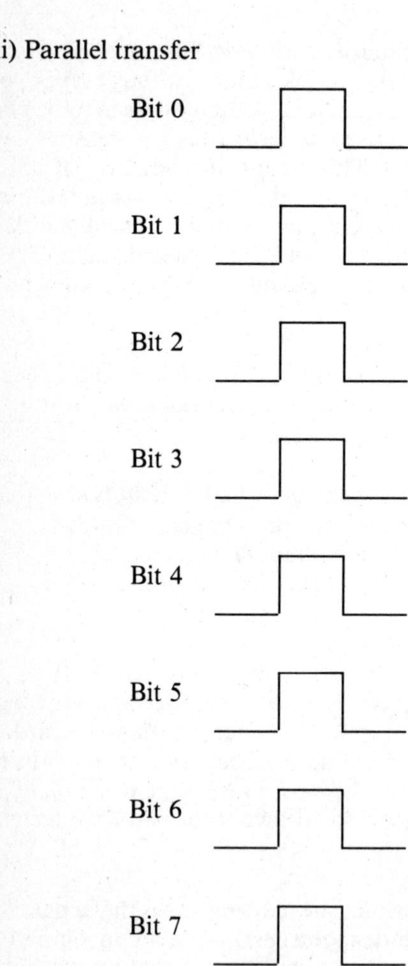

Fig. 9.1 Serial and Parallel Transfer

In a similar manner just one printed circuit board can also accommodate an expansion port, and a disk drive port as well. This certainly helps to keep the cost of production down; the 25-pin D-type connector usually included with an RS-232 interface is relatively expensive. Indeed, an RS-232 interface often increases the cost of a machine by many tens of pounds.

There are two such types of interface in general use which we will consider here – the *Centronics* interface and the *general purpose interface bus* (GPIB), otherwise usually known as the Hewlett Packard Interface Bus (HPIB – because they thought up the idea), or even more commonly the IEEE-488.

9.2 The General Purpose Interface Bus: IEEE-488

The General Purpose Interface Bus was mainly developed and standardized by the Hewlett Packard company; they required some sort of suitable interface to connect together the various pieces of electronic test equipment. Some means were needed to transfer data, and also provide for automatic control. The standard provides for bit-parallel (which means byte-serial) communications. In fact, up to fifteen different devices can be on the bus, and the interconnecting cable can be up to 20 meters in length.

In fact, the GPIB is defined in standards issued by both the American National Standards Institute (ANSI), known as ANSI MC 1.1-1975, and by the Institute of Electrical and Electronics Engineers (IEEE), known as IEEE Std 488-1975.

The bus consists of 24 lines. Sixteen of these are used as signal lines, divided into three groups. The first group contains eight signal lines that make up the *data bus* (one signal line for each bit of a byte, remember). Then there are five signal lines which make up the *general interface management bus*, and finally three signal lines which make the *data byte transfer control bus*.

In addition to these sixteen signal lines, there are seven ground lines. Finally, there is one line which is designated as a *shield*.

We will look at each of these groups of pins in turn.

The Data Bus

There are eight data lines, DIO1-8 (Data Input/Output). DIO1 is the least significant bit. i.e. bit 0, and DIO8 is the most significant (bit 7).

The pins used are numbers 1 to 4, and 13 to 16, i.e.:

Data line	Pin number
DIO1	1
DIO2	2
DIO3	3
DIO4	4
DIO5	13
DIO6	14
DIO7	15
DIO8	16

The General Interface Management Bus

This consists of five signal lines. They are as follows:

Pin 5. End Or Identity (EOI).
This pin serves two functions. It is used to indicate the last byte of data, when there are many bytes being transfered. Also, if this signal line is on when the ATN (see below) signal line is also on, it causes a polling sequence to be executed.

Pin 9. Interface Clear (IFC).
When on, this line signals the system to reset to a known starting state.

Pin 10. Service Request (SRQ).
This line is used as a sort of interrupt; if a device needs some attention, it turns this line on.

Pin 11. Attention (ATN).
This signal line is set or cleared by the controlling device. If it is set to on, it indicates that the data on the Data I/O bus is an interface message, not a device-dependent message.

Pin 17. Remote Enable (REN).
If this is off, all devices on the bus should be in local mode. However, if it is turned on, it enables remote operation of any devices on the bus.

The Data Byte Transfer Control Bus

Pin 6. Data Valid (DAV).
If this signal line is on, it indicates that the data on the data bus is valid, and is available to be used by any devices on the bus.

Pin 7. Not Ready For Data (NRFD).

If this signal line is low, it indicates that the receiving device or devices are not ready; conversely, if it is high then it indicates that all of the devices are ready to receive.

Pin 8. Not Data Accepted (NDAC).

This signal line is used to indicate whether or not the receiving devices which were to have accepted the data, have done so. If it is low, then they have not done so; however, the line will be pulled high when all of the devices have accepted the data.

The Ground Lines

There are seven ground lines, which are each used as grounds for the following signal lines:

Pin 18. Data Valid (DAV) ground.

Pin 19. Not Ready For Data (NRFD) ground.

Pin 20. Not Data Accepted (NDAC) ground.

Pin 21. Interface Clear (IFC) ground.

Pin 22. Service Request (SRQ) ground.

Pin 23. Attention (ATN) ground.

Pin 24. Logic ground.

Finally, pin 12 is used as a shield.

Operation of the GPIB

You will have probably noticed when discussing the RS-232, and other similar communications interface standards, that we have only ever talked of having two devices connected together at any one time – i.e. DTE connected to DCE. There has been no mention of having, say, three or four devices connected together via the RS-232. Indeed, the standards do not cater for this type of situation.

However, the General Purpose Interface Bus is entirely different in this respect. As mentioned previously, up to fifteen devices can be connected together on the bus. A sort of *network* can be built up, with each device connected to each of the data bus lines, and each of the data byte transfer control and general interface management bus lines.

Of course, most of these devices will probably be different; we will usually have one controlling device, which can also send and receive. We may have other devices, however, which can only send, or only receive, or maybe both send and receive.

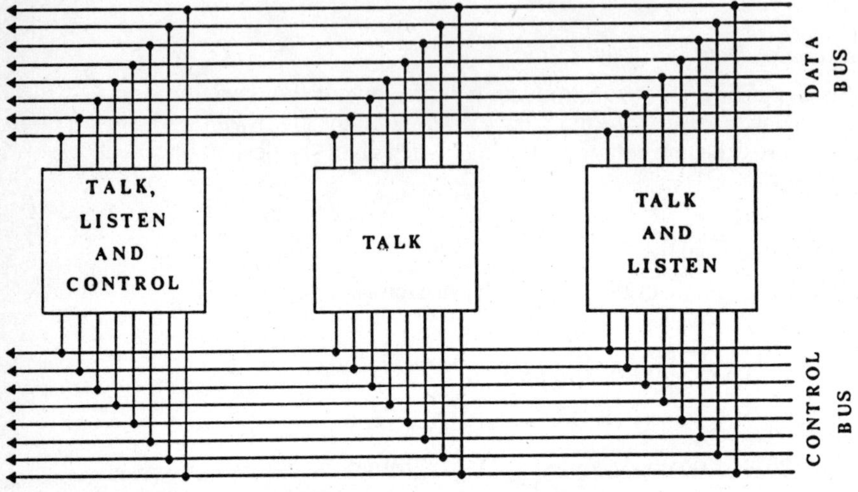

Fig. 9.2 A Net of Devices on the GPIB

You will probably begin to realize that the operation of the GPIB can be quite complex. There will be many different combinations of all the bus lines described, indicating different conditions and functions. This chapter will not seek to give an exhaustive explanation of the standard, but will hope to give some insight into its workings.

The standard specifies that the GPIB interface can have up to ten functions incorporated into it. We have already considered three of these above – the functions of *controller*, *talker* (i.e. able to transmit), and *listener* (i.e. able to receive). There are, however, others as well. These ten functions are:

Controller	C
Talker	T
Listener	L
Source Handshake	SH
Acceptor Handshake	AH
Device Clear	DC
Device Trigger	DT
Parallel Poll	PP
Service Request	SR
Remote Local	RL

Of course, not all of these functions need to be incorporated into any one device. For we could, as in the example above, have a device which only talks, or listens. Normally, however, you would not expect more than one device to be a controller.

These ten functions will now be described in some detail.

The Ten Interface Functions

i) Controller C

If a device is a controller, it means that the device can initiate such things as commands and addresses over the the interface; by this means a controller can, as you would expect, control other devices on the interface. The signal line Attention (ATN) will be ON when the controller is sending commands.

ii) Talker T

As well as the Talker (T) function, there is an Extended Talker (TE) function as well. The function is used to send device-dependent data over the interface.

iii) Listener L

In a similar fashion to the Talker function, the Listener (L) function is also accompanied by an Extended Listener (LE) function. The function enables a device on the interface to receive device-dependent data.

iv) Source Handshake SH

You will remember the idea of *handshaking* from the RS-232; the GPIB also uses the same idea. The source handshake function is, as the name implies, the handshaking function which controls the data transfer. A device with source handshake would be connected to one or more other devices with Acceptor Handshake function (see below).

v) Acceptor Handshake AH

This function is required by a device to be able to receive data from a device with Source Handshake function.

vi) Device Clear DC

This function allows either a single device, or a number of devices on the interface, to be cleared or reset.

vii) Device Trigger DT

In a similar way to Device Clear above, the Device Trigger function allows either a single device, or a number of devices on the interface, to have their operations started.

viii) Parallel Poll PP

Normally, the operation of *polling* takes place serially. Polling is used for a controlling device, for example, to have a look around to see what is going on. In a *serial poll*, the device would have to look at each of the other devices on the interface in turn. However, with the GPIB, it is possible to use the eight data lines DIO1 – DIO8 as eight separate polling lines; thus in the *parallel poll* system up to eight different devices can be identified.

ix) Service Request SR

This function is basically used by a device on the interface to ask the controlling device for some attention.

x) Remote Local RL

We may have the situation where a device has a choice of input; both the interface it is connected to , and also some kind of input from the device itself, like a keyboard. This function, then, allows the device to select whether the input is to come from the interface (i.e. Remote), or the keyboard (i.e. Local).

The General Purpose Interface Bus in Operation

You are probably by now (quite justifiably) feeling most bewildered by the idea of the GPIB; do not worry, for unless you are an electronics engineer you will probably never have to interface with it – unless it is set up ready for you!

The GPIB has quite a complex sequence of operation as far as the handshaking goes; also, the sixteen available control lines can be used in many different permutations to indicate different control functions. For instance, we can obviously transfer a byte of data, for that is what the interface is really all about, by using the eight data lines DIO1 – DIO8. However, these data lines can also, under some circumstances, be used for remote message coding; so too for the other eight control lines. It would be necessary, for a complete understanding of the General Purpose Interface Bus, to refer to the actual standards produced.

We next consider another type of parallel interface – and one which you are much more likely to come across and have to use in daily life. However, it is much more straightforward than the GPIB, and is quite standard in its connections. It is the *Centronics interface*.

9.3 The Centronics Parallel Interface

The most common type of interface, of either the serial or parallel type, to find included with a microcomputer is the *Centronics style parallel interface*. It is also quite common to find that printer manufacturers will build their printers, especially the cheaper models in their range, with a Centronics interface as standard; an RS-232 interface will have to be purchased and fitted separately.

This makes the Centronics interface most popular and easy to use, for unlike the RS-232 interface, the wiring and types of plugs are in most cases quite standard. (Although never take this for granted, as exceptions always occur!).

The interface uses 36 signal lines, although as with the RS-232's possible 25 signal lines, not all of these will normally be used. In fact, normally just eleven signal lines are needed, although this is a minimum, and some printers may use more.These are split into three groups:

eight signal lines are used for the *data bus*

at least two signal lines are used as control lines

one line is used as the *ground*.

We will now consider a typical pin configuration for a range of popular printers, although as stated the use of some of the pins may differ between manufacturers. Generally not all of the following pins will be used.

Centronics Pin Connections

Pin no.	*Return pin*	*Signal*	*From CPU*	*From Printer*
1	19	STROBE	X	
2	20	DATA1	X	
3	21	DATA2	X	
4	22	DATA3	X	
5	23	DATA4	X	
6	24	DATA5	X	
7	25	DATA6	X	
8	26	DATA7	X	
9	27	DATA8	X	
10	28	ACKNLG		X
11	29	BUSY		X
12	30	PE		X
13	–	SLCT		X
14	–	AUTO	X	
		FEED XT		
15	–	Not Connected		

16	–	0V		X
17	–	CHASSIS GROUND		X
18	–	+5V		X
19/ 30	–	Signal Grounds		
31	–	$\overline{\text{INT}}$	X	
32	–	$\overline{\text{ERROR}}$		X
33	–	Ground		
34	–	Not Connected		
35	–	+5V		X
36	–	$\overline{\text{SLCT IN}}$	X	

Pin Descriptions

Pin 1. STROBE

This signal line is used to provide the strobe pulse for data entry. A normal strobe, or clock, signal line would change from LOW to HIGH to indicate that data is on the line, and can be read. However, the bar over the top of STROBE indicates that this position is reversed – the signal line is HIGH in its normal condition, and a transition from HIGH to LOW indicates that data is on the line.

Pins 2-9. DATA1-8

These eight data lines are used to indicate the values of the eight bits of each byte – the bit is logic "1" when the data line is HIGH, and logic "0" when the line is LOW.

Pin 10. ACKNWLG

This is the *acknowledge* signal line. When it is in a LOW state, it indicates that the printer has has received the data, and is ready to receive the next lot of data.

Pin 11. BUSY

You may remember the hardware handshaking lines used in RS-232, such as RTS, CTS, DSR and DTR. This is the equivalent for the Centronics interface.

The printer indicates that it is not ready to receive data by pulling this line HIGH; if the signal line is LOW, then the printer is ready to receive data.

Thus there are three cases when this signal line may be HIGH:

i) during data entry
ii) when the printer is off line
iii) when there is an error condition

Pin 12. PE
This signal line is used by the printer to indicate *printer empty* – i.e. that it has
run out of paper.

Pin 13. SLCT
This line is pulled up to +5V at a load of 3.3 k ohms.

Pin 14. AUTO FEED XT
This signal line is used, by the CPU, to indicate a *hardware linefeed* to the
printer. When this line is LOW , (notice the bar above the name), the printer
should feed the paper by one line, after finishing printing the current line.

Pin 15. Not Connected

Pin 16. 0V
This is set to the LOGIC GROUND 0V LEVEL by the printer.

Pin 17. CHASSIS GROUND.
This line is connected directly to the chassis of the printer.

Pin 18. +5V.
The printer provides a direct +5V supply on this line.

Pins 19-30. Signal Grounds
Normally the data lines, and signal lines, use a common ground. However,
facility is made for twisted pair lines, where each data line or signal line has its
own ground line.

Pin 31. INT
This signal line can be used by the CPU as a *hardware initialize*. A LOW
condition will cause the printer to be reset to its initial condition, and clear its
input buffer.

Pin 32. ERROR
This signal line is used by the printer to indicate that some error condition has
occurred, e.g. the printer has run out of paper, or is just off line, or some other
error.

Pin 33. GND
This is another ground signal line, like pins 19-30.

Pin 34. Not Connected.

Pin 35.
This is sometimes another +5V supply line.

Pin 36. SLCT IN
If the CPU uses this signal line, a LOW condition indicates that the printer is selected.

Centronics Connectors

The standard connector for the Centronics interface is an *Amphenol*-type 36 pin plug or socket. Normally, a printer with a Centronics interface will be fitted with a female connector; a microcomputer would thus be fitted with a male connector.

However, as mentioned previously, some microcomputers, especially the cheaper, home variety, may not be fitted with a 36-pin Amphenol style connector; instead, an *edge connector* will be used. As its name implies, an edge connector fits directly onto the edge of the printed circuit board, which will be visible from the back of the microcomputer. This, of course, saves on the cost of manufacture of the equipment.

In fact, the standard type of edge connector which is suitable for the purpose has only 34 pins, and not the 36 of the usual connector. However, this does not matter, since not all of the 36 pins will normally be used. Normally pins 18 and 36 are missed out, the rest being connected one-to-one.

Functioning of the interface

The interface functions in a straightforward manner, as described in principle in earlier chapters. The data is presented on the eight-wide data bus as one byte of data, i.e. eight bits simultaneously. When the data is on the line, the STROBE signal line is changed from HIGH to LOW. Of course, a check should be made each time that the hardware handshaking line BUSY (pin 11) is LOW – a HIGH condition indicates that the printer is not ready.

Although the Centronics interface is relatively standard, there are, unfortunately, sometimes slight variations in the use of some signal lines (although the important ten lines, the eight line data bus, and the two signal lines BUSY and STROBE, always use the same pins). For instance, some printers (as described above) use line 14 as a hardware line feed signal line. If such a printer is connected to a device which does not utilize this facility, but has this signal line permanently connected to ground, then the printer will always see this signal line as being LOW, and will thus always add an extra line feed at the end of each line. This will probably not be what is required, but the situation can be remedied quite simply by disconnecting the line (e.g. by cutting it, if necessary!).

CHAPTER 10

Local Area Networks

10.1 Introduction

The term Local Area Network (or LAN for short) has been on people's lips for two or three years now; although widely misused or misiniterpreted by some, it has been the favourite subject of conversation for most people regarding themselves to be "in the know" for some time now. The term is in fact not a precise one at all, and is still growing and adapting to the situation surrounding it.

The term is, fortunately, fairly concise in its self-explanation. Whereas the greater part of this book has dealt so far with the strict problem of connecting just one device to another (say, a computer to a printer), by means of some interface (whether this be RS-232, RS-449, Centronics, or whatever), we now consider how to go about stringing another one into the circuit, and another, and so on. One thing is, so far, certain: there is no standardization in sight for either the theoretical or practical aspects of constructing a local area network. Far from having the relatively happy situation of a standard laid down by a relevant august body (such as we have, no matter all its pitfalls, with the RS-232-C specification), any standards to be set for local area networks will be decided by market considerations, and which manufacturer can gain the greatest foothold. Up until the present day the play has sometimes been rather dirty; this gives an indication of how high the stakes are in sales of suitable systems over the next few years or decade.

The converse of the Local Area Network has been considered in passing in other parts of the book – Wide Area or Long Haul Networks. Electronic mail (such as Telecom Gold, Easylink and One to One) is an example of the latter. In these cases, an effective solution for low-cost data transfer is found to be the use of conventional telephone lines and modems (or acoustic couplers). However, this necessitates low transfer rates for the data.

The principle of a Local Area Network, although not the name, has been around for a long time. Consider the problem faced by conventional mainframe or supermini computer manufacturers such as IBM or Digital Equipment Corporation (DEC). Until the recent expansion of processing power of microcomputers (which can now match that of some minicomputers), the conventional answer for a company requiring high processing power was to use a minicomputer, such as DEC's PDP or VAX range. Thus, the computing system would be based on one central processor, along with hard disk drives, tape backup and so forth. To this would need to be connected as many terminals as necessary, as well as printers, plotters, etc. Thus a network of devices naturally grew up around a central processing machine.

The idea of, and need for, relatively inexpensive and adaptable local area networks arose with the increased power and range of abilities of desk-top microcomputers. It is quite commonplace nowadays for such machines to boast features unheard of just a few years ago, such as microprocessors matching mini and mainframe processors in their speeds and abilities, large amounts of RAM (hundreds of kilobytes), and hard disks, such as the Winchester variety, of very large capacity (at least ten or twenty megabytes). With such processing power, and such storage capacity, the desktop microcomputer can rival a minicomputer.

Of course the disadvantage has been that one workstation (used by perhaps just one individual) can harbour much information that other individuals, at other workstations, may need to have access to as well. The most wasteful solution has often been to have copies of the same files at every workstation. But there are two obvious disadvantages:

i) this approach is tremendously wasteful on storage capacity; the same file may be duplicated many times

ii) unless rigorous updating standards are applied, the same file on different machines will soon start to differ in its contents, as different users update different records.

A far more satisfactory approach would be for each workstation, with perhaps its own large-capacity hard disk storage system, to keep files uniquely; but it should be possible for other workstations to access these files and update as necessary. In this way, both of the above points can be dealt with. There will be no duplication of storage space for the same file, and since any file is unique the problems of updating different versions does not arise.

There may be other advantages in connecting all the devices in one office, or block of offices, together. Expensive resources other than hard disks, such as high quality or high speed printers, may be accessed by all workstations. (This saves having to carry machines from one room to another, in order to plug them into such devices!)

Out of such needs have arisen Local Area Networks. Being "local" does actually present some advantages – for instance, there is now no need to rely on existing lines of communication (such as the telephone system). Since the system is local, and typically in the same office or building, it is quite practicable and inexpensive to lay down specific lines for the purpose. Thus conventional data transmission rates can easily be raised manyfold. There is now no constriction of low baud rates, using RS-232 interfaces, to connect via a telephone line (remember in this country that it is not generally possible to use baud rates of higher than 1200); indeed, there is no need to use RS-232, or even RS-449/RS-422, interfaces at all. The way is open for new communications standards – if such a thing is possible when rival manufacturers go to war.

10.2 Local Area Network Configurations

Local Area Network configurations tend to fall into three different types, *star*, *ring*, or *bus*.

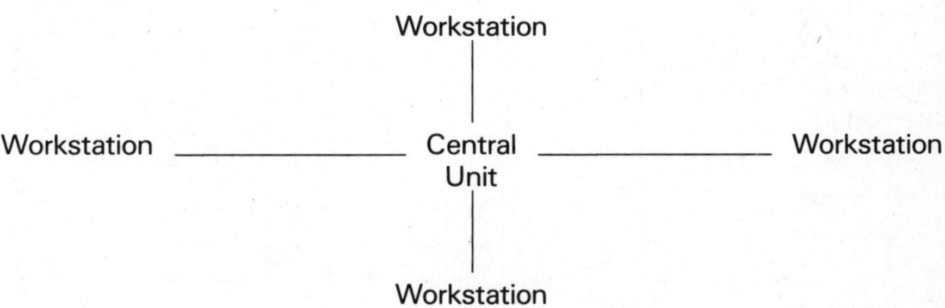

Fig. 10.1 Star type configuration for LANs

One of the earliest types of Local Area Networks utilized a particular sort of PABX (Private Automatic Branch Exchange), commonly used to route speech lines over an internal telephone network, to route data channels as well. Now, an ordinary, dedicated, telephone line with a modem can operate at data transfer rates of up to about 16,000 baud. However, the newer digital systems can operate at far higher speeds – typically up to 80,000 baud.

This type of Local Area Network thus uses a star configuration – the PABX sits in the centre of the system, with all other devices connected to it, as in Fig. 10.1. Thus the central unit contains all the necessary storage and processing power to control what is going on – switching the traffic of data on the communications lines as and when necessary, for instance.

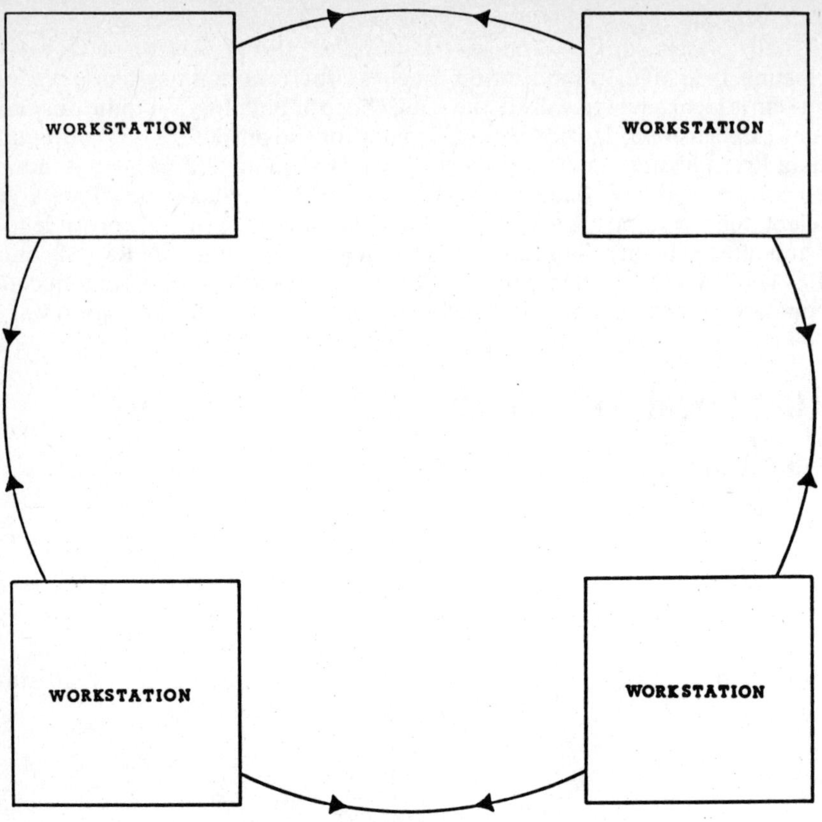

Fig. 10.2 Ring type configuration for LANs

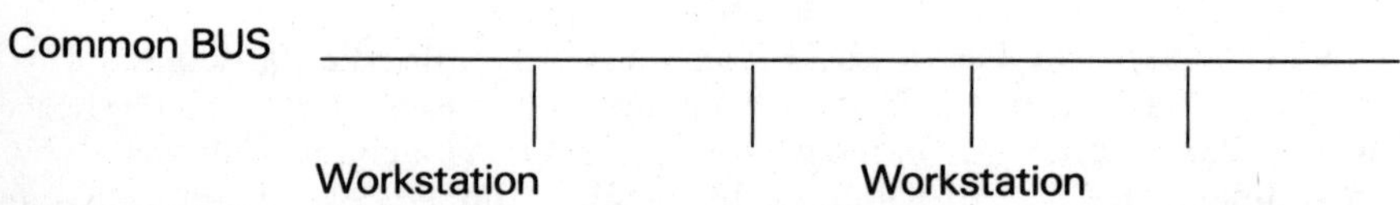

Fig. 10.3 Bus type configuration for LANs

However, the two most common, and most widely quoted, types of Local Area Networks use the other two configurations—the ring and the bus. Although there are many types of ring networks, the most common is the *Cambridge Ring*; in direct competition to this is one of the alternative bus systems, *Ethernet*. This is a product which has been developed by the giant Xerox company, and has found great favour amongst many users.

10.3 Ethernet

The Ethernet type of Local Area Network does not use conventional signal lines, such as telephone wires or cable of the type used for RS-232 transmission, but rather uses co-axial cable instead. This means an immediate advantage in the speed at which it is possible to transmit data – up to 10 million bits per second! Unlike the star configuration outlined above, there is no central controller to look after the management of the network – instead, each device in the net is of equal status.

One immediate problem of any networking system is how to control the data transfer. There may be (and probably will be) many devices on the network at the same time, each wishing to transmit at much the same time. How is a successful and safe system to be constructed?

One answer would be for each workstation to be "polled" in turn, by a central controller for instance, to see whether it needs to transmit data. However, Ethernet uses a different system. All of the devices in the network are allowed to transmit at any time they wish, with the proviso that they first "listen" to the line to see if it is busy. Only when the line is not busy is the device allowed to transmit data.

Of course it may be, in extreme cases of bad luck, that two devices start to transmit at exactly the same time. This is catered for by the Ethernet system by equipping devices with "collision detection", whereby if a collision is detected by a transmitting device it simply stops, waits for the line to go quiet, and then tries again. Likewise, any receiving device on the network which detects a collision simply ignores that data.

The system of collision detection carries the unfortunate name of CSMA/CD – which stands for Carrier Sense Multiple Access with Collision Detection.

10.4 Local Area Networks – The Future.

LAN's are certainly here to stay, as more and more manufacturers support them at many different levels – both with operating systems and application programs. For instance, one of the most standard operating systems for 16-bit microcomputers (for who nowadays expects a true standard to emerge?) is Microsoft's MS-DOS (and its close equivalent, as specified by IBM for its range of personal computers, PC-DOS). This has now been enhanced by a networking version – MS-NET, with which applications software companies strive to make their products compatible.

Likewise most software houses with business applications programs, such as wordprocessors or spreadsheets, or indeed integrated packages, are bringing out networking versions for their clients. There is, again, a natural demand from users for such a networking system. There are, for instance, many powerful database programs on the market with sophisticated programming languages. With these many users will have built up extensive databases for their businesses; they will now want other users, in the same office perhaps, to be able to share the same database files with ease.

Hopefully, however, standards (which are all too lacking in the microcomputer marketplace) will emerge for Local Area Networks to help ease the end-user into the systems with as little pain, and as little strain on the bank balance, as possible.

For further information, you may wish to consult another Sigma publication "Low Cost Local Area Networks", by S.P. Bridges; published in May, 1986.

CHAPTER 11

File Transfer Techniques

You will have seen by now just how to go about communicating successfully with many types of devices, such as microcomputers and printers. However, the emphasis up until now has been on how to send or receive that vital chunk of information – the byte of data. Little consideration has yet been given to some aspects of actually encoding data into these bytes, although you will have come across by now the ideas behind a standard character set, such as the ASCII or EBCDIC character table.

We will now look at what it means to have to transfer a file of data; how this can be accomplished in different ways, and the reasons why different methods do have to be used.

Although any type of communications system could be used, we will in general be considering the use of a bit-serial, asynchronous system, such as the RS-232.

Let us first consider some of the problems associated with file transfer. It is all very well for us to pick up a byte of data, and transmit it down the line to some receiving device. How is the receiving device to know what to do with this data, or where to put it? This answer is straightforward for a terminal (or terminal emulator) – everything which is received is displayed on the screen. Now, this is fine when we are interacting with, say, a host computer system. However, we will in many cases wish to transfer a file of data. This may just be text, as in a list of names and addresses. However, it may be pure binary data, like the object code of a program to run on a computer.

Of course, our file transfer may be implicit in its instruction. For instance, producing a listing on a printer is really a file transfer of the text of the file via, say, anRS-232, into the printer. The only thing a printer knows how to do is to print out characters, and this it will try to do no matter what is thrown at it.

11.1 ASCII Text

In most cases then, as in the example of producing a listing of, perhaps, a letter, we are concerned with *text data* – i.e. the letters, numbers, and other characters you see on a keyboard. Now, we have seen already the need to standardize on

some sort of character set of codes for all of these symbols. You will remember
that our basic chunk of data for storing information is the *byte*, which is made
up of eight *bits* of data, each of which can be 0 or 1. This would give us a
maximum of 2^8 different combinations, or 256 different codes. Now, the
ASCII character set requires just seven of these bits to be used – there is always
one left over. However, this still gives us 128 combinations, which is enough for
all our letters, numbers and other symbols. We can now specify that each
character is assigned a *unique code*; our codes run from 0 to 127, so we could
(according to the ASCII character set) assign the number 48 to the character
"0", 49 to the character "1", etc.

The standardization is essential, in order that a receiving device will know what
a sending device is talking about. For instance, if we send the code "76" to a
printer (which is the character "L" in the ASCII character set), we want it to
print out on a piece of paper the character "L". If we were connected up to a
printer that thought we were sending EBCDIC code, instead of ASCII, then it
would actually print out the character "<", which is not what we wanted!

But given that both transmitting and receiving devices agree on the character
translation being used, text transfer is quite straightforward. As well as
producing listings on a printer, we can also quite easily transfer files of text from
one computer to another. The essential ingredient which makes this possible are
the extra codes in the ASCII character set – the *control codes*. For if you look at
the ASCII character table in the Appendix in the back of the book, you will see
that any character we send will always lie in the range from 20 hexadecimal (32
decimal), which is a space, up to 7E hexadecimal (126 decimal). However, the
other characters can be used to instruct our receiving device, whether it is a
printer or microcomputer, just what to do.

As an example, consider a small file of names and addresses held as a text file
in a microcomputer:

```
FRED JONES, 1 HIGH STREET, WINCHESTER.
JOHN SMITH, 22 ACACIA AVENUE, MILTON KEYNES.
PETER WRIGHT, 121 OLD LANE, CARDIFF.
```

Then, to transmit this file of information, our program needs to just read the
characters one by one, translate them into their corresponding ASCII code, and
send them down the RS-232 line. Thus the first character, in decimal, will be 70,
the next will be 82, and so forth. What happens at the end of the line? We would
probably like the next record to be on a new line if it is to be printed. A printer
will also need to know that it is to start each new record at the leftmost position
on the paper. This is the function of two *control codes* in the ASCII character
set – *linefeed*, to go onto a new line, and *carriage return*, to indicate that the
printer should start in the leftmost column.

Now, both linefeed and carriage return lie in the area below20 hexadecimal in the ASCII set – so a printer knows that they are control codes, and are not to be printed. There is one more useful control character we may require for printing – the *formfeed*. For imagine we are printing out a series of letters. Then we would probably like to have each new letter starting on a new page. This is the purpose of the formfeed control code – it instructs the printer to advance on enough lines (i.e. repeated linefeeds) until it is at the top of a new page. How is the printer to know when it is at the top of a page? Computer paper is a standard size, both in width and length. So, provided the paper is set to the top correctly at the start of printing, the printer can remember how many lines it has printed, and thus know how many more lines there are to go to make up a complete page.

We may not,of course, be sending this file to a printer – it may be going into another computer. In this case, if this computer is set up as a terminal, it will be displaying the lines on the screen just like a printer. However, whilst this enables us to read the file, the data will be lost when it scrolls off the top of the screen, which will not be much use to us. What is required is some system of *capturing* the data, as it is received, and writing it back out to another file, say to a diskette.

There are a number of ways that this can be accomplished. If we are using a terminal emulation package, like the ones described in a later chapter, they will probably offer a file capture system. Thus by a pressing a function key, or entering in some unique command string, the terminal emulator will redirect the input to disk, as well as (or instead of) displaying the data on the screen. Alternatively, we have written a simple program to accept the file and save it to disk, or we may use an operating system command. For instance, in CP/M we could use

```
A>PIP FILE.TXT=AUX:
```

where the auxiliary port is defined as the RS-232, FILE.TXT is the name of the file to be received into and PIP is the CP/M command for file copying (Peripheral Interchange Program).

What will these systems for receiving files make of the control codes we are sending, like carriage return and linefeed? Well, normally they will not mind; the will usually just save the control code as well as the text characters. In some cases, superfluous characters such as linefeed and formfeed will be discarded – a carriage return may be all that is needed to signify the end of a record. Thus if we receive the list of names and addresses into a file, this is what it would actually look like:

```
FRED JONES, 1 HIGH STREET, WINCHESTER.<CR><LF>JOHN
SMITH, 22 ACACIA AVENUE, MILTON KEYNES.<CR><LF>
PETER WRIGHT,121 OLD LANE, CARDIFF.<CR><LF>
```

where <CR> is the control code for carriage return (0D hexadecimal), and <LF> is the control code for linefeed (0A hexadecimal).

How will the receiving program know that we have reached the end of the file? This normally does not matter with a printer; the sending device will know when the last record is sent, and the printer will just wait for more input. We can always tear off the sheet of paper, to take it away with us! But our receiving program will "hang"—it will still be waiting for more records. This is where another control code in the ASCII character set comes in handy—the *end of file* marker. The control code that is normally used is called CONTROL Z; it is actually designated as SUBSTITUTE (SUB, which is 1A in hexadecimal, or 26 decimal) in the ASCII table. An explanation of "control Z" follows below; for the moment, we will consider the use of this particular control code:

Whenever the receiving program receives this control code, it will recognize that it is the end of file marker—the last record has been sent. Thus it will know that it is safe to close the file which was open for input, and return to the controlling program. It may also often save this control code as well; this may prove useful later on when we wish to do more processing on this file. Thus our complete received file now looks like:

```
FRED JONES, 1 HIGH STREET, WINCHESTER.<CR><LF>JOHN
SMITH, 22 ACACIA AVENUE, MILTON KEYNES.<CR><LF>
PETER WRIGHT,121 OLD LANE, CARDIFF.<CR><LF><EOF>
```

A Note on Control Characters
You may have realized that, since the control codes are all quite distinct from the everyday characters of a keyboard, there appears to be no way of accessing most of them, should the need arise. Of course one of them, carriage return, has its own key—the RETURN key. So too does the control code right at the top of the ASCII table—delete. You will also have noticed several other keys normally found on a computer keyboard, such as ESC, CLR and possibly ALT. There is also one called, surprisingly enough, CONTROL.

The way the control key works is very simple—you press *and hold down* the control key, and then press another key at the same time. What now happens is that 40 hexadecimal (i.e. 64 decimal) is subtracted from the ASCII character value of the key you pressed. For instance, if you had pressed CTRL and Z, then since Z in the ASCII table has the value 5A hexadecimal, the resultant value is 1A hexadecimal, which is our end of file marker! Similarly, there are a number of other multiple keypresses which yield common control codes:

CTRL M is a Carriage Return
CTRL J is a Linefeed
CTRL L is a Formfeed.

The use of control characters does not stop in these cursor-positioning codes, for it extends also to the subject of *software handshaking*. You will remember that we use the XON and XOFF characters, which in the ASCII table are DC1 and DC3. Of course you will see now that these are just CTRL Q (XON) and CTRL S (XOFF). If your terminal emulator is set up correctly, CTRL G (which is BELL) will make a bleep!

11.2 Binary Data

Up to now we have considered text data – alphabetic, numeric and other punctuation-type characters. These leave plenty of space in the ASCII table for control codes, so we can look after what is going on. You will remember our file of data, by now saved on a disk is:

```
FRED JONES, 1 HIGH STREET, WINCHESTER.<CR><LF>JOHN
SMITH, 22 ACACIA AVENUE, MILTON KEYNES.<CR><LF>
PETER WRIGHT,121 OLD LANE, CARDIFF.<CR><LF><EOF>
```

This is not actually what it would appear like in the file, whether the file is on a disk or in the RAM memory of the computer. It would actually be a string of bytes of data; each byte being a string of 0's and 1's. So the file would actually start off:

```
01000110010100100100010001
```

and so on. In fact this is just the first three letters, F, R, and E! For F, in binary, is 01000110; that is, 0100 0110 or 46 hexadecimal (70 decimal). Similarly, R is 52 hexadecimal, or 01010010 in binary.

You can see that it would take a long time to print out the contents of the bytes of the whole file in binary, which is why a format such as hexadecimal is favoured. In fact, the whole file in hexadecimal, a "hex dump", would be as follows:

```
46524520 4A4F4E532C2031204849474748205354524545542
C2057494E43484855355445522E0D0A4A4F484E20534D4953
482C2032322041434341434941204156454E4E55452C204
D494C544F4E204B45594E45532E0D0A50455544552205752
4947485442C3132312 04F4C44204C414E452C2043415244 4
94646 2E0D0A1A
```

Although this may still look quite cumbersome to the layman, it is certainly a lot easier to digest and a lot shorter than binary. With a little practice, you can quite easily learn to pick your way through such a file, decoding the hexadecimal into characters or control codes. For instance, the pairs of carriage returns-linefeeds (i.e. 0D0A) can be spotted quite easily.

Of course this is, at the end of the day, just binary data. It is only because we know, and the printer knows, that characters and control codes are encoded into it according to the ASCII character set that some meaning can be deduced from it. However, there may be occasion to transfer *pure binary data*, which has nothing to do with ASCII. For instance, consider the *object code* of a program, which is to run on a microprocessor. This may have been produced by a compiler from a high level language, such as Cobol, C, or BASIC. Or it may have been produced by an assembler from assembly language source code; for instance, consider a small program written in assembler for, say, a Z80 microprocessor:

```
LDA A,13
INC  A
PUSH BC
POP  IX
LD   A,(DE)
RET
```

Then the assembler will produce (here listed as a hexadecimal dump) the following object code:

```
3E0D3CC5DDE11AC9
```

where the byte of data C5, for instance, is the translation of PUSH BC. We may wish to send the object code of this small, and quite useless, program to another microcomputer; it may be a device based on the Z80 microprocessor, and we may wish to run the program on it. How is this to be done?

You will see that if we were to use our faithful text file transfer system above, all kinds of things would go wrong. It would think that the first character, 3E, was a ">", the second was a carriage return, and so on until the last but one which it would interpret as an end of file marker!

This is the inherent problem of transferring binary data; there is no room left for any control codes to instruct the receiving device as to what is going on, for all of the 256 possible values for a byte may be taken up. There are two ways around the problem: we can either devise another system for sending this data, in some other encoded format, or we can use extra hardware handshaking signal lines to control the transfer.

In the latter case, it would be possible to use a clocked, synchronous serial or parallel system, with handshake lines for bit transfer synchronization and so on. But this would clearly not be possible with an asynchronous system such as RS-232. Fortunately other systems have been devised; we will look at one of these systems next.

11.3 Motorola S-Format

You will remember the little Z80 assembler program we wished to transfer to another computer:

```
LD    A,13
INC   A
PUSH  BC
POP   IX
LD    A,(DE)
RET
```

The assembler subsequently produced the following object code:

```
3E0D3CC5DDE11AC9
```

This is of course a hexadecimal representation. In binary, it would be:

```
0011 1110 0000 1101 0011 1100 1100 0101 1101 1101
1110 0001 0001 1010 1100 1001
```

We need to be able to transfer this, as a file, via the RS-232 interface. There are several ways of doing this, but perhaps the most popular and common is by using *Motorola S-format records*. This is a most ingenious, but simple, system whereby all the data is re-encoded as *text*, and then transmitted as separate lines of known length. There is also an element of error-checking built in to the system.

The basic idea is to transmit the file of binary data in its hexadecimal printout form; thus the first byte of data, which is 00111110 in binary, or 3E in hexadecimal, is actually transmitted as *two* bytes of data, i.e. first a "3", and then an "E", in ASCII! Thus we actually transmit (in hexadecimal):

```
3345
```

or in binary:

```
0011 0011 0100 0101
```

Now, as well as encoding each byte of data into *two bytes of text*, the record structure has some more features as follows:

i)   the first character of each record is an "S"

ii) the second character of each record is the *record type*:
     0 for a header record, 1 for a data record with a two byte address, 2 for a data record with a three byte address, or 9 for the end record

iii) the next two characters are *the number of bytes that are to follow*, (call this number X)

iv)   the next four characters for a data record of type 1 (or six characters for a data record of type 2) are the *load address of the first byte of the record*

v)   *there then follow 2*X characters (remember, there are two characters for each byte, and there are X bytes)*

vi)   *finally, there are two characters which are the checksum*

The Header Record

This is usually as follows:

    S00600000484445521B

and note that this is the actual text which is transmitted.

As stated, the first character is an "S". The next character is a "0", which means that it is a header record. We next have two characters — 06 — which are the number of bytes to follow. Thus there are six bytes of data to come, which means twelve characters (there being two characters per byte). The next four characters are an address (which can be ignored for a header record); this address is set, as you can see, to 0000.

We now come to the data itself. There are eight characters to go, or four bytes. Now, the last byte is the checksum, so there are three actual data bytes. These are:

    48, 44, and 52

which, if you look in the ASCII table, you will see are:

    "H", "D", and "R"

    i.e. "header"!

Finally, we have the checksum. You may remember from RS-232 the idea of *parity* — setting a spare bit to a "1" or a "0" depending on how many 1's or 0's there are. This is an alternative idea — all the values of the bytes are added up, and the checksum is set so that it, added to the sum of the numbers, equals FF hexadecimal, or 255 decimal (disregarding any carries in the addition). i.e. in the header record, we have

    06 + 00 + 00 + 48 + 44 + 52 = E4

(hexadecimal arithmetic, remember!) so the checksum + E4 must equal FF. Thus the checksum is 1B.

Rather more strictly speaking, the checksum is *the one's complement of the sum of the count byte, the address bytes, and the data bytes, carries above one being discarded.*

The Trailer Record

This is usually as follows:

```
S9030000FC
```

which is much shorter and easier! Here we just have "S" as the first character, "9" to signify a trailer record, 03 as the number of bytes to follow, an address of 0000, and a checksum of FF. Note that

$$03 + 00 + 00 + FC = FF \text{ in hexadecimal.}$$

The data record

Remember the object code of our little program above; it was:

```
3E0D3CC5DDE11AC9
```

All we have to decide now is where we want it to go in the receiving device, i.e. the address in memory where it is to go. Of course the receiving device may ignore this address, and place the code wherever it wants; but the possibility is there for us to place the code.

For instance, we might know that executable code for the machine should start at an address in the memory map of the microcomputer of, say, D000 hex. Then our data record should be:

```
S10BD0003E0D3CC5DDE11AC9AA
```

Thus, the complete file to be transmitted will be as follows:

```
S00600004844521B
S10BD0003E0D3CC5DDE11AC9AA
S9030000FC
```

How will the receiving device interpret the incoming records? All it has to do is to work backwards; the processing goes something like this:

START:

    wait for an "S"

    wait for next character

    is it a "9"?

    if so, it is the end

    is it a "1"? (or "2"–we will not deal with that case here) if not, go back to the beginning

    receive next character, and *translate this back as one byte of data* remember this byte – it is the count of the number of characters following in this record

    receive next two characters

    now translate these back as one byte of data this is the high-order byte of the address

    receive next two characters

    translate these again: this is the low-order byte of the address

    from now on, receive two characters at a time, translate them into one byte of data, and save them in ram, beginning at the specified start address, until all the characters have been received. Also keep a tally of the sum of all these characters, as well as the address and byte count

    receive the last two characters – the checksum byte is the checksum correct? If so, go back to the start if not, break out – there has been an error

The program illustrated above is very small. We would normally expect to see something like this:

```
S00600004844521BS123000003861F86107F00709749967
2B700FDCE01A5DF56DF54BDFA98CE020071F717D6C3S123
00207253D417D717CE41FD96037C0057260671FB1772041
7750117A700088C43FD263CS1230040E87230174F5FDDEE
DDF0CC43EDFD00F6CE007BBD41FD860697B6CE43F0DFBFC
E3CS123006043FDDFC3CE47F6867EA700A706CC4316ED0
1CC4310ED07720570397EF851C80161S1230080444C2020
4F46463A7EF991C801440858535245433A397F0070CE02E
8DF54BDFAD1S12300A098CE025E71F717D67253D417D717
CC40DE3C189603750117A7000818380926F100S12300C08
60597B6CCF987DDBFCC40EDDDC14F9781978497799764 7E
```

```
F8517F0049860597875S12300E0B6CE00BFCCF987ED00BD4
20E00F17EF061CE463F3CCEFAD0DF8FCC0166DD8DDEA3S1
2301008FA60008DF8F38A700083CDE8D09DF8D26ED38CE4
62FFF00C13FC610CE445EBD9DS1230120FD45CE479BFF47
093FC60ACE446EBDFD45CE46D9FF46D13FC60ACE4478BDF
D4551S1230140CE46F9FF4783CE466EFF4780CE46B5FF47
86CE47A63FC61FCE4482BDFD457F00F7S12301608B39C70
0464E2043414C433A720F5E7EF54D47A947A6FF97FECFFD
0546EA471E79S123018046E347824763BDFD0596A3949C2
712BDFD26969C260ECE0097C6056201057EFD05S12301A0
09BDFD2639DFEC8D62CC43EDDDF6398D23DFEC3820058D1
C388D121893F6D3EE9DS12301C0183CCE42203C20218D0A
38201AEC00DDEC080839360797FC32DDF8DFFA398DF4A9S
12301E020058DF038EE00DFECDEEC8C400024098D19DCEC
93EED3F6183CDEFADCF8369621S1230200FC0632398DCE3
88DC420BA9CEE25049CF02543CE0546BD42E4DFEE960375
011719S1230220D60375011718DFF09CEC23ED8D25DEEE8
D5ADCF093EEC3000104D7F4DEF6960323S1230240750117
A7000896037500117A700087A00F426EB7230173971FB177
20417398C4003S1230260002503EC00398D249603750117
D60320E236378DE918DFF23332398DE1DDF2399BS123028
0378DDB334D39368DD51632393CDF54BDF9FDD6FDD772BD
FAACC103270CC605D7AFS12302A0B6CCF977DDC17EF061B
DFA98D67271F71753D417D7173839BDF9FD7EF04AD640A7
S12302C02B17C1052613D7B696492707BD425C0F18D9BDF
4707EF0657EF459CCF987DD75S12302E0BF71FD707F0049
3920205472616E736D697474696E6700C801419A2053524
54327S12303003A9664367F0064BDF917329764BDFA2786
10D67AC102270A48D67BC10227037ED6S1230320F851979
13900533030363030303034383434353231425339303330
303030464380S1230340530000000000000000000000000
0000000000000000000000000000000000000000046S1230360
00000000000000000000000000000000000000000000000
000000000000000079S12303800000000000000000000000
1684F0444444448B3081392F028B07C40FCB30C1392F90S
12303A002CB0739CE47F3867EA703A709CC432DED04CC43
36ED0A7205704F5F97679766CDS10403C0B7810739CE47F
3867EA703A709CC432DED04CC4336ED0A7205704F5F9767
9766CDS9030000FC
```

Notice that our Motorola format file may be transmitted in the following way (that is, carriage returns and linefeeds may be included in the stream of data):

```
S00600004844521B<CR><LF>
S10BD0003E0D3CC5DDE11AC9AA<CR><LF>
S9030000FC<CR><LF><EOF>
```

Thus we have accomplished what we set out to, for we are now back in the happy state of being able to use control characters, such as carriage return, linefeed and control Z, once again.

Of course, an immediate disadvantage is the a file in Motorola S-format is more than twice as long as its binary counterpart. However, this really only means that it will take twice as long to transmit, which is a compromise we are probably only too happy to have to take.

CHAPTER 12

Other Handshaking and File Transfer Techniques

So far, we have looked at the most common methods of handshaking and file transfer. For instance, our handshaking has been confined to one software method, using XON and XOFF control codes, and one hardware method, using the RTS and CTS signal lines of the RS-232 interface. There are, naturally, many other methods as well; some are in quite common usage, whilst others may be custom-designed for a particular purpose, or piece of apparatus.

We will first take a look at one method which combines a software handshake method, embellishes it with error-correcting ideas, and combines the whole into a file transfer technique.

12.1 XMODEM (ETX/ACK)

ETX/ACK sounds rather similar to XON/XOFF; indeed, if you have looked at the ASCII character set you may have noticed that ETX and ACK are two more control codes, like XON and XOFF. In actual fact, ETX and ACK are not the only control codes used in this method of handshaking: there are two more as well. These are the control codes that will be used:

Dec	Hex	Character	Control Code	Meaning
2	2	STX	<CTRL>B	Start of Text
3	3	ETX	<CTRL>C	End of Text
6	6	ACK	<CTRL>F	Acknowledge
21	15	NAK	<CTRL>U	Negative Acknowledge

Let us see how this system works. We will first consider the operation from the viewpoint of the transmitting device. (Any communications method could be used – normally it would be RS-232).

The sending device first sends an STX (Start of Text); it now waits for the receiving device to send back an ACK – Acknowledge.

When the ACK has been received, the sending device knows that there is something on the other end of the line, which should be ready to receive the data. The file transfer technique now differs from ones we have previously considered, for the data is not sent as one long stream, or continuous flow of records. Instead, the file is split up into a number of *blocks*, which are transmitted one by one.

Thus the sending device now transmits the first block of data. Its composition is as follows:

    16 byte filename
    2 byte block number
    1 byte block length
    data bytes
    2 byte checksum

There can be from 0 to 128 bytes of data; so the block length also ranges from 0 to 128. You may remember the idea of a *checksum* from the description of an alternative method – Motorola S-Format. In the S-Format records, the checksum is just one byte, and is the one's complement of the sum of the data, length, and address bytes. However, in this case the checksum is *two bytes in length*, and is the sum of all the data bytes.

A zero block length means that it is the *end of the file*.

So the transmitting device sends this record. When this is done, it waits for a reply from the receiving device. The receiving device will reply with either an ETX, an ACK or a NAK.

An ETX (End of Text) means that the transmitting device should *abort* the operation. If the receiving device has replied with a NAK (negative acknowledge), it means that something went wrong with the file transfer; for instance, it may have found that the checksum was not correct for the data bytes it had received. There may have been a break in the signal line, or a bit may have been dropped. In this case the transmitting device should try again – it just sends the same block of data. Thus this process can be repeated until the receiving device has taken in the block of data correctly.

Alternatively, the receiving device may have replied with an ACK (Acknowledge), which means that all is fine, and the block was received successfully. In this case the sending device can:

either send a new block of data,

or, if it is the end of the file, send a zero length block to signify that this is so.

What about the sequence of operations from the point of view of the receiving device? They are as follows:

First the receiving device waits for an STX (Start of Text). When this is received, if it is all set to go, it responds with an ACK. From this you will see that the receiving device should be set up and ready before the sending device is, or at least at the same time. Otherwise it may miss the first STX.

It now receives the block of data, as outlined above. It can now check for a number of things:

i) If it is not the first block. it must check that the filenamc is the same

ii) If it is not the first block. it must check that the block number is consecutive.

In these two cases, if there is any error, it should reply with an ETX (End of Text) and abort the operation.

It can also check for one other case: is the checksum correct? If it is, it can reply by sending an ACK; this will prompt the transmitting device into sending the next block of data. Alternatively, if the checksum is not correct, it should reply with a NAK, thus indicating that it would like the same block to be sent once more.

Finally, it should check the block length. If it is not zero, then another block of data will be on its way. Conversely, if the block length is zero, it is the end of the file.

You will notice that this method is rather longer and more involved than just sending a straight ASCII text file; there is a greater overhead of non-data bytes, such as the file name, block number and checksum. There is also arbitrary stopping and starting whilst sending blocks of data, which is quite independent of the receiving capabilities of the device which is accepting the data. Compare this to a straight file transfer, where the only stopping and starting is the handshaking, which is directly controlled by the receiving device.

The big advantage is, of course, that there is complete confidence in the data being transfered correctly, or at least an error being shown up if there is one. Furthermore, both this method and any other, such as straight file transfer, which use the RS-232, can also have a deeper level of error checking; for remember that each byte of data can itself have a parity bit, which the receiving device can check, to give us even greater confidence that the data has been correctly transfered.

12.2 Other Hardware Handshaking in the RS-232

There are also many different ways of configuring hardware handshaking systems. As far as the RS-232 interface goes, we have mainly considered RTS/CTS handshaking. You will remember with this that the Data Terminal Equipment (DTE) can pull the Request To Send (RTS) signal line – which is pin 4 – either high or low depending on whether it is ready or not to receive data. Likewise, Data Communications Equipment (DCE) pulls its handshaking signal line, Clear To Send (CTS) high or low depending on whether it is ready to receive data. Now, in the RS-232 interface itself you will have noticed many other signal lines which obviously have something to do with hardware handshaking. They have all been discussed in principle; how do they operate in practice?

There are three other important pins in the RS-232 which are often used for hardware handshaking. They are:

Pin 6, Data Set Ready (DSR)

Pin 8, Data Carrier Detect (DCD) and

Pin 20, Data Terminal Ready (DTR).

Data Set Ready and Data Carrier Detect are both controlled by the Data Communications Equipment, whereas Data Terminal Ready is controlled by the Data Terminal Equipment.

Some devices may simply use the DSR and DTR lines as hardware handshake lines, instead of the RTS and CTS signal lines; i.e. we have DSR/DTR handshaking. Alternatively, you may come across the case (and this is quite common) of a device which uses RTS/CTS for the handshaking, but also requires other signal lines to be in a particular state.

For instance, consider Data Terminal Equipment, which uses the RTS signal line for hardware handshaking. Now, it may also always set its DTR signal line ON (and this will stay on all the time); however, in return it requires the Data Communications Equipment to set its DSR signal line ON as well. Now, the DCE may not use the DSR signal line in its RS-232 interface – what is to be done?

It is actually quite simple. All we have to do is *to connect together the DSR and DTR pins* (pins 6 and 20) *of the DTE's RS-232 interface*:

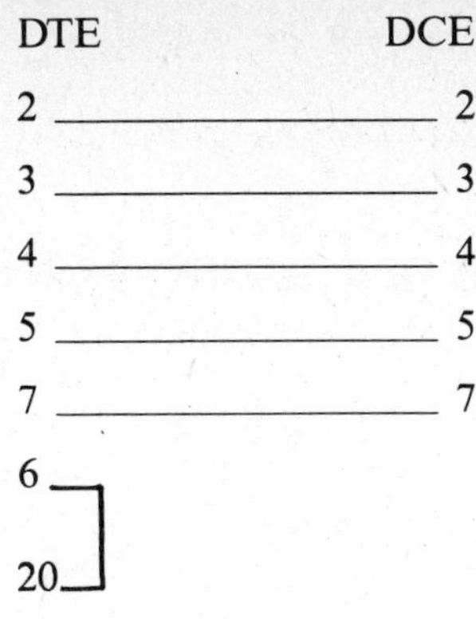

Fig. 12.1

This means that whenever the DTE puts DTR (pin 20) HIGH, then the DSR signal line (pin 6) also goes high, thus effectively fooling the DTE into thinking that the DCE has itself pulled DSR high.

You may also find, especially when connecting up to modems, that the DCE uses the Data Carrier Detect (DCD – pin 8) signal line instead of DSR. Indeed, even worse, combinations of all these methods may be used. For instance, consider the RS-232 interface for one popular range of home microcomputers – the Amstrad CPC 464/664/6128.

Consider this interface connected to a modem; The microcomputer will then be acting as a terminal emulator. The terminal will be the DTE, and the modem the DCE. Now, when the terminal sends to the modem, RTS/CTS handshaking is used. That is, when the terminal is ready to transmit it turns the RTS signal line on, and the modem, when it is ready to receive data, turns on the CTS signal line. The terminal will only send data when the CTS line is on.

However, the case is slightly different when the modem transmits data to the terminal. For when the modem wishes to send data, it turns on the DCD signal line; when the terminal is ready to receive data, *it* turns on the DTR signal line. The modem will only transmit data when the DTR signal line is on.

Thus we have effectively two different sorts of handshaking going on – RTS/CTS when the terminal is sending data to the modem, and DCD/DTR when the modem is, in turn, sending data back to the terminal.

Of course we still do not have to confine ourselves to using the RS-232 interface, or the RS449/423/422, or even the GPIB interface! There are many occasions, and many devices, which call for some unusual, possibly even customized, interface and corresponding handshaking method. We will illustrate the point by considering one such system below.

12.3 An Example of Custom Hardware Handshaking

Let us now set up a system using five lines:

one transmit line

one receive line

two handshaking lines and

one signal ground line.

Furthermore, we will configure a system to allow us to transfer data from a device A to a device B, or from B to A.

So far, you might think that this is not too different from, say, an RS-232 interface. However, we will now set up our own bit transfer and handshaking system, as follows.

Let us first look at the signal lines (we will leave out the ground line) in their rest states; device A has a transmit line Ta, and a handshake line Ha. Similarly, device B has a transmit line Tb (which is the receive line for device A), and a handshake line Hb.

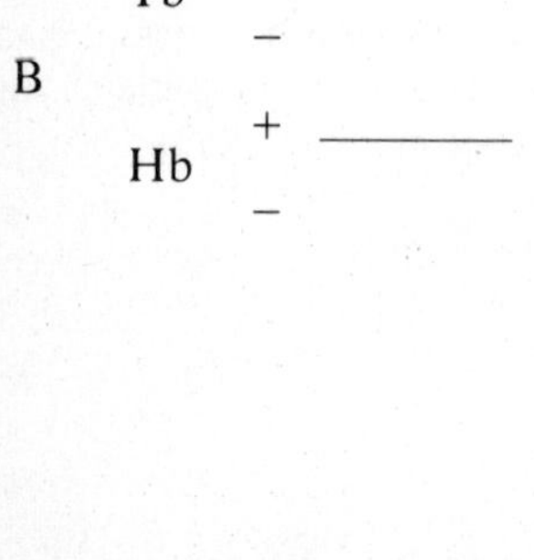

Fig. 12.2

Suppose now that device A wishes to transmit a bit to device A. This bit is either 1 or 0, i.e. high or low. Suppose it is low. Then the transmit line for A, Ta, will go to negative:

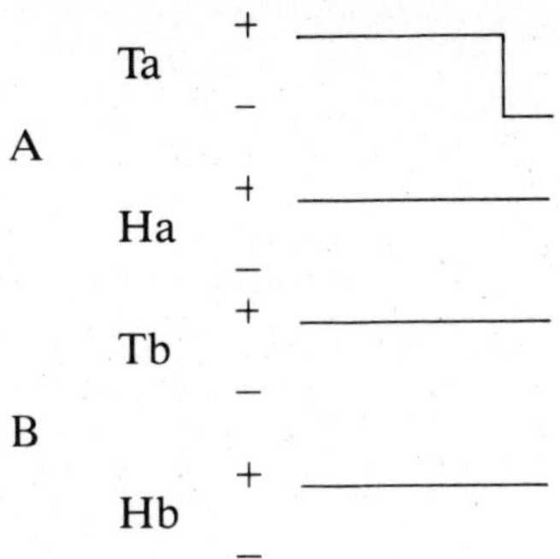

Fig. 12.3

In order to signal this event to device B, A will also *toggle* its handshake line — from high to low:

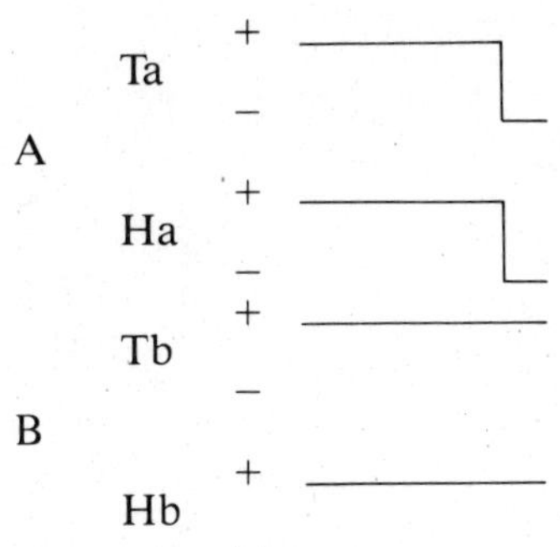

Fig. 12.4

Device B, meanwhile, will be watching A's handshake line, for a change to indicate that A is sending some data. When B sees this change in Ha, it knows a bit of information is on the line Ta; it now indicates to A that it has noticed the change in the handshaking line Ha by toggling *its* handshake line, Hb, from HIGH to LOW:

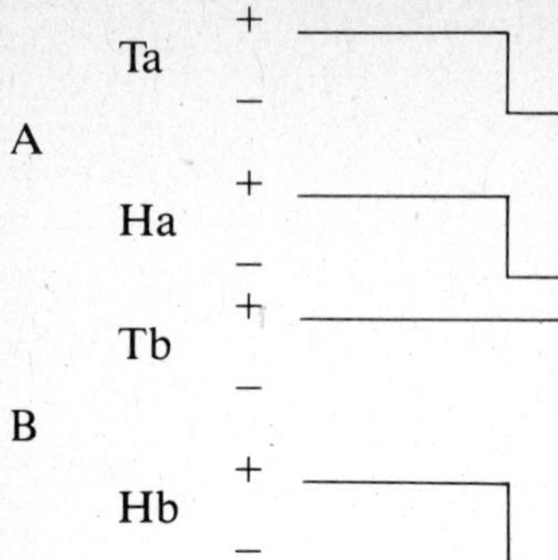

Fig. 12.5

When this is done, B can now read the value of the bit on the transmit line Ta. B indicates to A that it has finished reading the data by toggling its handshake line back up to high again:

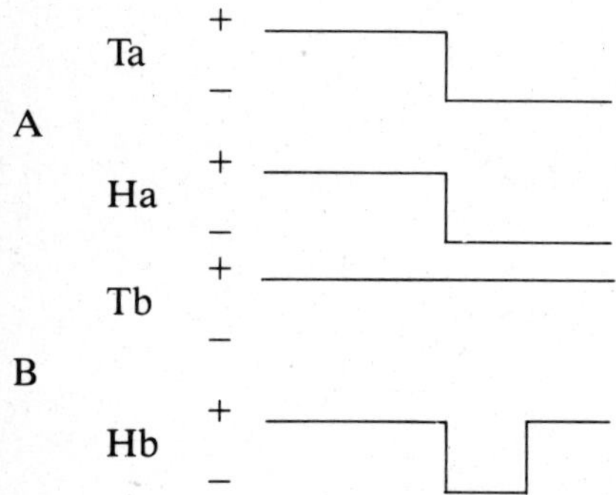

Fig. 12.6

Conversely, A will be watching B's handshake line to see when B has read the bit of data; it knows that this has been accomplished when Hb goes from HIGH to LOW and back to HIGH again. Thus it can now reset its handshake line, and its data transmit line, back to high:

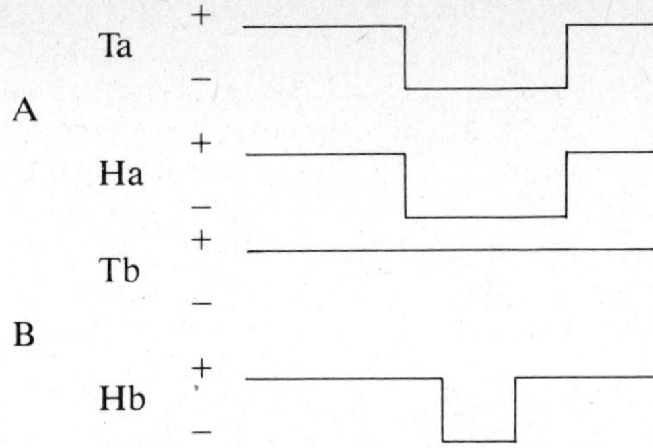

Fig. 12.7

Thus one bit of data has been successfully transferred. Of course, this first bit need not have been a "0"– it might have been a "1". In this case, there would have actually been no change on the transmit line Ta; it would have stayed the same, in the HIGH position. This highlights the need for the handshake line (really a *clock* line),for the situation would then have been like this:

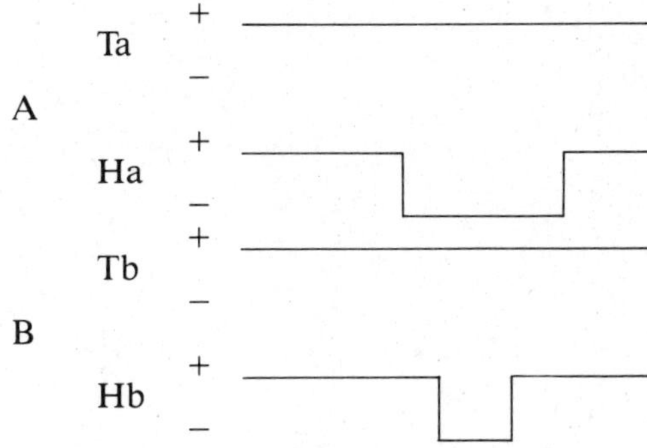

Fig. 12.8

Of course, our device B can transmit data back to A in exactly the same way; indicating the bit value on its transmit line Tb, pulling its handshake line Hb from high to low, waiting for A's handshake line, Ha, to go from high to low and back to high, and then resetting its signal lines.

Thus this whole process can be repeated over again to transmit a whole string of bits of data.

What are the advantages and disadvantages of such a system of data transfer? You may have already noticed several advantages; there is no need to specify beforehand any data transmission rate – this is all controlled entirely by the two devices toggling their handshake, or clock, signal lines. Indeed, the system is most suited to some applications in that both devices have a say in the speed of data transfer, for the transmitting device cannot send a new bit of information until the receiving device indicates that it is ready, and the transmitting device can, in turn, take as long as it likes over sending bits. One other advantage is that there are also no wasted bits, such as the start and stop bits of RS-232.

What, then, are the disadvantages? There are three main ones – the first is that this interface is non-standard. Whilst this is fine for a specialized application, it gives no flexibility in, say, the choice of machines used, unless these too utilize this interface. Secondly, the interface is, by the very nature of its handshaking system, rather slow in data transfer. For whereas in a system such as RS-232 the data can be bundled together into small packets – a byte of data surrounded by a start bit and a stop bit – this process uses a most laborious method of signalling, confirming and resetting lines for each bit.

Finally, the interface does require the two handshaking lines; this would make it unsuitable for situations where the data has to be transferred over, say, the telephone network.

CHAPTER 13

The Musical Instrument Digital Interface

The subject matter of this book has been, until now, aimed fairly and squarely around conventional computer communications problems, techniques, and answers; how to connect a computer to another computer, for instance, or how to connect a computer to a printer. We now consider a similar problem in a different field – how to connect a computer to an electronic musical instrument, or indeed how to connect one electronic musical instrument to another. Whilst the problem is of a slightly different nature, it is most illuminating in that the solution has been built upon the standard techniques already covered in earlier chapters, and pleasing notice has been taken of earlier pitfalls of non-standardization amongst manufacturers.

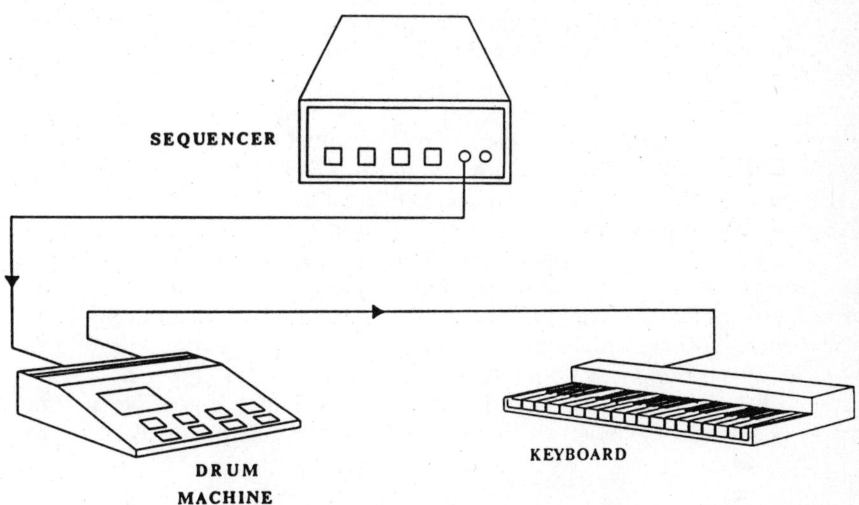

Fig. 13.1 Connecting Musical Instruments Together

Why should any such interfacing be necessary? As you might expect, the problem has arisen only recently with the advent of sophisticated electronic equipment in music such as synthesisers and drum machines. Early problems arose with, for instance, the need for a drum machine (which produces a regular rhythm) to be synchronized to a sequencer (which plays a set pattern of notes over and over again). Unless one can "drive" the other, synchronization will be lost and the drums and keyboards will go out of step with each other.

This early problem lead to the immediate solution of a single synchronizing signal line to connect say, as in the above example, a drum machine to a sequencer. Thus a pulse produced from the drum machine can cause the sequencer to play a note; the two will thus stay perfectly in step. This bears remarkable similarity already to, say, a clock pulse signal line used in conventional computer communications.

13.1 The MIDI Specification

However, electronic keyboards have become more and more complex, and the interfacing needs correspondingly more and more widespread and necessary. For instance, there is a need for machines to start and stop each other, to play different preset patterns at the same time, and even to play each other by passing information on the note pitch and filter cut-off settings. It is fortunate that the electronic keyboard manufacturers saw the good sense to sit down at an early stage and construct a common standard for musical equipment interfacing. The companies involved were two major manufacturers from the United States, SCI and Oberheim, and some of the principle manufacturers from Japan. The result in April 1983 was the Musical Instrument Digital Interface (or MIDI for short) specification version 1.0.

The MIDI specification aims to cater for a broad range of needs in interfacing musical instruments. You will see how similar it is to another, most common, interfacing specification we have considered in great detail already – the RS-232. However, it is not compatible, as it has several more advanced features: the rate of data transfer is much higher than that allowed by RS-232 for instance. More importantly MIDI can cater for up to sixteen separate channels (although only one wire, as with RS-232, is actually used for transmitting). Thus one device can control many others independently; indeed, some electronic keyboards nowadays boast a "split keyboard", which means that the upper and lower halves of the keyboard can be set to different sounds. Thus it is possible in some cases to drive the two halves of the keyboard as separate channels from the MIDI interface.

13.2 MIDI Hardware Connectors

You will remember, if you have studied the previous chapters on the RS-232 and RS-449 interfaces, the type of connectors used – 25 pin or 37 pin "D-types". However, the MIDI interface specification needs only two lines, for the current loop transmit line (which means that there is one transmit line and one return, or ground, line). Additionally, the connecting lead is shielded throughout; the shield is connected to earth.

Thus the connector specified for the MIDI interface on the electronic keyboard is a DIN 5-pin 180 degree female panel mount receptacle. There will normally be at least two – one labelled "MIDI IN" and the other labelled "MIDI OUT". Additionally, there may be a third labelled "MIDI THRU", which provides a direct copy of data coming in from the MIDI IN socket.

Two of the pins of the MIDI interface are not used – pins 1 and 3. Pins 4 and 5 are used as the current loop transmit lines, and pin 2 is connected to the shield and earth. Thus, there is an essential difference between the MIDI interface and, say, the RS-232 interface: with the RS-232, transmit and receive functions are all catered for with one connector (as well as secondary transmit and receive lines, and control signal lines), but the MIDI connector is for one-way only data transfer. However, its simplicity does make for much easier connecting leads – which is fortunate as the average musician is probably not too adept at using a soldering iron!

Connecting cables are specified as having a maximum length of 50 feet (15 meters), like the RS-232 specification. The cable should be terminated on both ends by a corresponding 5-pin DIN male plug. The type of cable used should be shielded twisted pair, with the shield connected to pin 2 of the plug at both ends.

13.3 The MIDI Interface – Data Transmission

The MIDI interface specifies a system of data transfer which will be most familiar to those now well versed in RS-232 technology. However, you may remember that the maximum (but rarely achieved) baud rate for RS-232 is 19200; this is found to be too slow for interconnecting musical instruments, as a large amount of data (note pitch and duration, for instance) may need to be shifted around. This is the reason for MIDI using current loop circuits (as with the RS-422 standard), and as a result the baud rate is raised to 31250 (+ or – 1%). Again perhaps fortunately for musicians, the transmission parameters are fixed exactly for MIDI – there is no provision for altering the baud rate for instance.

In exactly the same way as RS-232, the MIDI interface uses *asynchronous* data transfer, with one start bit, eight data bits, and one stop bit. As with the baud rate, there is no provision for using different arrangements of the number of data bits or stop bits.

```
Baud rate                           31250
Start bits                              1
Data bits                               8
Stop bits                               1
```

Fig. 13.2 MIDI Interface Setup

As far as the electrical characteristics of the circuits go, the current loop types
used have a nominal current flow of 5mA. Note that data is inverted in the same
sense as RS-232; that is, logical 0 is CURRENT ON. The interface operates at
a voltage of 5V. This, you will note, is again in the range for RS-232; indeed, you
may have already noticed that the MIDI interface is most like the RS-422.

13.4 Communicating with the MIDI interface

MIDI communicates, as with other conventional computer communications
systems, by means of bytes of data (each byte consisting of eight bits); indeed,
the packets of data tend to come in *words*. Unfortunately, a word has a different
length (i.e. contains a different number of bytes) for different machines and
manufacturers. A word may be just two bytes long, or four bytes for some
mainframe computers (or some of the latest microprocessors).

The MIDI interface uses a word length of three bytes, although, in exceptional
cases,a longer word length is used. There are two categories of commands
carried by the MIDI interface – *system* commands and *channel* commands.

Channel Commands

Imagine the situation of a number of musical instruments, perhaps a drum
machine and two or three keyboards, with one of the instruments playing the
master role and controlling the rest. It would be unacceptable if, every time the
master instrument instructed one device to do something, all of the others did
the same thing as well. For this reason the MIDI interface can cater for up to
sixteen channels, and each device in the chain can respond to just one of these
channels. Thus the master instrument can now control up to sixteen channels,
and thus sixteen separate instruments, independently.

Thus channel commands are used to tell a specific instrument just what to play
and when to play it. There are now also many keyboards which boast touch-
sensitive keys; in this case information has to be relayed also about the velocity
associated with each note.

System Commands

There are three types of system commands:

System Common commands
System Real Time commands, and
System Exclusive commands

In the case of System Common, the commands are intended for all of the devices connected together in the network. Remember that this may often be a desirable thing, for instance when wishing to select a particular sequence, and starting at a particular place in this sequence. There is also a facility for requesting analogue synthesisers (if they have the ability) to tune their oscillators!

System Real Time commands are again intended for all of the units in the network. They are generally used for synchronizing the whole system, by means of start, stop and timing clock commands. Additionally, there is an active sensing command, which if present means that the keyboard should take its commands from the MIDI network; otherwise, control reverts to the normal operation for the device, for instance taking key presses from the keyboard once again.

System Exclusive commands are used in conjunction with a particular manufacturer's unique identification code. Thus if a system exclusive command is sent, followed by a particular manufacturer's identification, then any data which follows will be obeyed only by that manufacturer's machine (if there is one in the network). Thus different types of machines from different manufacturers and with different capabilities can be catered for on the MIDI interface.

13.5 MIDI Data Format Examples

You will remember that the word size used is three bytes (except for one special case which will be covered later). The MIDI word is arranged as follows:

byte 1 is the *status byte*
byte 2 is a *data byte*
byte 3 is a *data byte*

For instance, the status bytes for System commands are as follows:

System Type	Binary Value	Hex Value	Action
Exclusive	1111 0000	F0	Dump follows
	1111 0001	F1	Undefined
	1111 0010	F2	Song posn pointer
	1111 0011	F3	Song select
Common	1111 0100	F4	Undefined
	1111 0101	F5	Undefined
	1111 0110	F6	Tune request
	1111 0111	F7	End of exclusive
	1111 1000	F8	Timing Clock
	1111 1001	F9	Undefined
	1111 1010	FA	Start
	1111 1011	FB	Continue
Real Time	1111 1100	FC	Stop
	1111 1101	FD	Undefined
	1111 1110	FE	Active sensing
	1111 1111	FF	System Reset

Fig. 13.3

Similarly, the status bytes for Channel commands are as follows (in all cases the low nibble of the status byte is the channel number, i.e. from 0H to FH):

High nibble Binary	Hex	Action
1000	8	Note off
1001	9	Note on
1010	A	Poly pressure
1011	B	Control change or mode message
1100	C	Programme change
1101	D	Channel pressure
1110	E	Pitch wheel

Fig. 13.4

The contents of the second and third bytes of the word, which are both data bytes, will depend on the status byte. For instance, consider the System Exclusive command Dump Follows (status byte F0). Then the second byte will be the *manufacturer's identification*, which should be in the range 0 to 127 decimal (0 to 7F hex, or 0000 to 0111 1111 binary). In this case, there may now follow any number of bytes of data.

Conversely, consider the Channel command NOTE OFF for channel 0 (which will thus have the status byte 80). Then the second byte will be the PITCH NUMBER, in the range 0 to 127 decimal (0 to 7F hex, or 0000 to 0111 1111 binary), where middle C has the value 60. The final, third, data byte will be the OFF VELOCITY, once again in the range 0 to 127 decimal (0 to 7F hex, or 0000 to 0111 1111 binary). The default value is 64.

Similarly, all other status bytes would have corresponding second and third data bytes, depending on use. These are all laid down in detail in the MIDI data format specification, version 1.0.

13.6 Using the MIDI Interface in Practice

I am sure that you will agree that all of the above information on connecting devices together seems fine in theory – but we could equally well be talking about any set of electronic equipment, and the problems of setting up standards in interfacing. It is quite obvious to most people that there is a real need for communications in general everyday computing circles, but what use is communications in the sphere of electronic musical equipment to most musicians, whether they are professionals or amateurs?

As is so often found to be the case, the inclusion of an open-ended, flexible interface on any piece of equipment opens up boundless possibilities to people with the imagination to see beyond the narrow confines of the original idea. Thus the MIDI interface has given rise to a great many uses and products. These fall into two distinct groups – the immediate possibilities of simply interfacing electronic musical equipment together (say, connecting a drum machine to a keyboard), and the exciting possibility of connecting a computer into the MIDI interface network, thus allowing the huge processing power of the computer to come into the system.

13.7 Interfacing Musical Equipment via MIDI

Let us consider the first possibility. At its very simplest, the MIDI interface allows us to connect a drum machine to a sequencer. As stated in a previous example, the two can now produce their respective sounds (the drum machine producing synthesised bass, snare, tom, and cymbal sounds, and the sequencer whatever sort of sounds the keyboard allows or you wish) whilst staying in perfect synchronization; the drum machine can be used to *trigger* the note playing of the sequencer.

Taking the idea one stage further, it should be possible for one device equipped with a MIDI device to actually play another one similarly equipped; thus one machine can be used to produce the sounds of another machine, actually out of that machine. What use is this feature? Consider the example of a drum machine connected to a synthesiser. Then, it is possible to actually play the drum sounds by means of hitting the keyboard of the synthesiser itself. Likewise, a sequencer on one synthesiser could produce the sounds on another synthesiser which is itself not equipped with a sequencer.

There are, naturally, limitations to the system, depending on the capabilities of the pieces of equipment in the MIDI network. For instance, some keyboards boast touch-sensitive or velocity-sensitive keyboards – so the MIDI interface will be carrying data relating to these two parameters. However, not all keyboards have these features; if you are interfaced to one that does not, it will simply not understand the data coming in from the MIDI interface.

13.8 Interfacing to a Computer via MIDI

Perhaps the most interesting possibilities arise from the idea of connecting a computer into the network by means of the MIDI interface. Even using a modest and relatively cheap home computer, such as a Sinclair Spectrum, Commodore 64 or Apple II, the available processing power of microprocessors and cheap RAM (which means large memory) opens up whole new fields. For instance,from the point of view of actually playing the music the computer can be used to run the whole show. Commercially available software offers sequencers (real time or step time) with capacities of many thousands of notes across many channels. But it does not stop there. It is possible to actually compose on the computer, with the music score displayed on the screen. The music can thus be edited by deleting, inserting or altering notes. At the end of the day the whole piece can be "dumped" to a mass storage device, such as a disk drive or cassette tape, for later use.

Even more exciting is the possibility of making a direct "digital recording" of what is being played on, say, an electronic synthesiser. All the data being received by the computer from the synthesiser via the MIDI interface can be "dumped" directly into RAM; thus, all necessary data concerning note pitch, length, voice change or pitch bend can be saved, so that the music can be played back at a later date exactly as it was originally. Of course it is not possible on a home microcomputer with relatively limited memory to save the complete data for more than a few hundred or a few thousand notes; but already more sophisticated computers, with larger available memory, can store all the necessary data for a far larger number. Perhaps one day your Long Playing record or Compact Disk will arrive in a microchip!

CHAPTER 14

Kermit Terminal Emulator and File Transfer Program

14.0 Introduction

With the growth in popularity, and usage, of communications packages on personal computers, there has been a corresponding growth in the number of packages available. One package which combines both terminal emulation and so-called "intelligent" file transfer is *Kermit*. There are three unusual aspects of this package. First,it is available for a very wide range of computers, and is not just limited to only IBM PC's and compatibles, but is also available for a variety of mainframes and minicomputers, from manufacturers such as Digital Equipment Corporation (DEC) with their range of VAX and PDP super-minis, IBM, Prime, Data General, and also non-MS-DOS eight-bit microcomputers such as the Apple II. Thus, sophisticated file transfer can easily be accomplished between computers of enormously varying power.

Secondly, Kermit uses its own particular brand of file transfer protocol. You may recall from previous chapters some of the considerations that need to be taken into account when transferring large files of data. The RS-232 protocol may be set such that each byte of data has a *parity bit* set – this will help in error-detection, but does not provide any "intelligence" for a file transfer system. In Chapter 12 a more intelligent file transfer protocol was described – *Xmodem*. In this system, if an error occurs during file transfer, the protocol allows for "having another go" – until it succeeds! Kermit, too, utilises this sort of idea. Kermit's file transfer protocol is rapidly gaining wide popularity, and consequent general acceptance as an "industry standard".

Thirdly, Kermit is an exceptionally cheap – or free! – package. It is one of many excellent packages offered by, in the United Kingdom, the IBM Personal Computer User Group. For a small joining fee many hundreds of packages of all descriptions are available at very little cost. Not only is the executable code provided, but also the source code! For the interested "hacker",this means that not only can the programs be updated to his or her own requirements, or bugs fixed, but that also the source may be studied to provide enlightenment on the workings of the package.

In return for all this hard work and information, the authors do ask people who have bought their package that if they feel pleased with the programs offered, then a voluntary sum of money be sent to the authors in appreciation.

14.1 Kermit-MS

The package we shall describe here is the one specifically designed for microcomputers running Microsoft's popular operating system MS-DOS, and specifically the IBM PC/XT/AT family (whose operating system is named PC-DOS). Kermit was developed at the Colombia University Centre for Computing Activities, U.S.A.

In the U.K., Kermit-MS is provided on two disks from the IBM PC User Group—disks numbered 207 and 208 in their range, in fact. These two disks contain all the files necessary to understand what is going on (by reading the various *help* and *document* files), to actually run the program (by invoking the executable file KERMIT.EXE), and to actually look at the source code of the program and rebuild the whole system, if necessary.

There are first a number of *help* files which maybe read before embarking on using the program—README.207 and README.208, which describe the package in brief outline, and also provide a description of the contents of each file on the respective disks; MSKERMIT.DOC, a lengthy document from the Kermit Users's Guide which goes into some detail about the package and its various functions; MSKERMIT.HLP, which provides a more concise outline of the operation of the program; MSBUILD.HLP, which provides information on "building" (assembling and linking all of the separate source modules into executable code) the program ; and MSMETA.HLP, which provides information on executing a command file to reconfigure the IBM keyboard for a particular usage.

14.2 Invoking Kermit

One nice feature of the Kermit package is that it is not necessary to enter the program to utilize its functions. For instance, you can *SEND* a file from Kermit either by entering the package, as described in the next paragraph, or just by invoking Kermit at the DOS command line level, and passing arguments to it (file names, or parameters) at the same time, i.e.

    A:\>kermit send fred.txt

However, the program can be executed in the normal PC-DOS fashion by typing in, at the DOS command A:\> (if you are running the program directly from the floppy disk, for instance):

```
A:\>kermit
```

The following will then be displayed:

```
IBM-PC Kermit-MS V2.27
Type ? for help
```

```
Kermit-MS>
```

You will notice that the normal DOS command prompt has been replaced by the new Kermit prompt `Kermit-MS>`. Also, the version number of the program is displayed (at the time of writing, version 2.27 is the latest available, although the documentation on the disk refers to version 2.26). Since it is always a good idea when using a new package for the first time to see what help is available, typing in a question mark thus:

```
Kermit-MS>?
```

(no carriage return is needed after the "?") displays a list of the available commands:

BYE	CLOSE	CONNECT	DEFINE
DELETE	DIRECTORY	DO	EXIT
FINISH	GET	HELP	LOCAL
LOG	LOGOUT	PUSH	QUIT
RECEIVE	REMOTE	RUN	SEND
SERVER	SET	SHOW	SPACE
STATUS	TAKE		

Some of these you will recognize as being fairly self-explanatory, whilst others may need some investigation first. However, simple help facility is provided at this level — by typing in a required command, and then a question mark, more information in the desired key input is displayed. Take, for example, the *SET* command. Typing in the following after the commmand prompt:

```
Kermit-MS>set?
```

(again, no carriage return is needed after the question mark), displays a list of parameters which may be configured using this command. The list starts:

```
BAUD rate
BELL
BLOCK-CHECK-TYPE
DEBUG
DEFAULT-DISK
```

and so forth.

14.3 Kermit Commands

We will now describe some of the Kermit commands in more detail, concentrating on ones which will be of more direct relevance to an inexperienced user.

Leaving Kermit to return to DOS

Before delving too deeply into the workings of a new package, it is always nice to know how to get out of it! This can be accomplished in three ways, by typing in either:

    Kermit-MS>quit

or

    Kermit-MS>exit

in order to return back to DOS. Note that these two commands may be shortened to just a single letter—"q" or "e".

Alternatively, the command

    Kermit-MS>push

can be used to invoke the MS-DOS command processor COMMAND.COM, and return to DOS. The advantage of using this method is that it is possible to return to DOS, and then subsequently come back into Kermit, without destroying Kermit's settings.

The DOS commands

Some useful DOS-type commands can also be accessed at the Kermit-MS level, like the normal *directory* command, to display a list of files in the current directory. Note that wild cards can be used, and a path name can be specified. Note also that because the question mark "?" is used for *help*, this is not available for the single character wild card, as in MS-DOS. Instead, the equals sign " = " is used.

We can also find information on the available disk space and status by using, appropriately enough, the *space* command.) This is just like the MS-DOS command CHKDSK).

Similarly, the command *delete* is used in the same way as the DOS command *del*, and *run* is used to invoke an MS-DOS.EXE or COM file.

The *show* command can be used to display informationon either the scan code settings for the keyboard, and also the macro settings being used. For instance, typing in:

Kermit-MS>sh k (which is an abbreviation for "show key")

will result in:

Press key:

Pressing any key now will cause the scan code of the relevant key and any definition set; for instance, pressing the *return key* would probably result in the following being displayed:

Scan code: 28
Definition:

The SET command

The next thing that we will probably wish to do is to set up the normal communications parameters for the RS-232 port – baud rate, parity, handshaking and so forth. This is accomplished, naturally enough, by using the *SET* command. For instance, we can set the baud rate to a required setting by typing in:

Kermit-MS>set baud 2400

or whatever is required.

Similarly, we can disable or enable Xon/Xoff handshaking for the terminal emulator by typing in:

Kermit-MS>set flow-control none

if we do not require software handshaking, or

Kermit-MS>set flow-control xon/xoff

if we do require it.

You will find with practice that these, and similar, commands, can be greatly shortened. For instance, the two examples above could equally well be typed in as:

Kermit-MS>set f n

and

Kermit-MS>set f x

Thus the normal RS-232 parameters can be set as required. In addition, there are one or two more parameters to be set before we can start to have some chance of successful communication. For instance, we may have more than one RS-232 – communications – port fitted into the expansion slots of the microcomputers. In this case, we use the command

    Kermit-MS>set port 1

to use com1 or aux, or whichever port is required.

One other parameter we may wish to set at this point is the *end of line* delimiter – which is normally set to carriage return. This we do by the command

    Kermit-MS>set end-of-line

or, more succinctly, just

    Kermit-MS>set end

However, we need now of course to type in the required character to act as a delimiter. But how is this to be done? If at any stage we become stuck over what to do next, Kermit provides a nice help facility – we simply type in a "?", e.g.

    Kermit-MS>set end?

which will display the message:

    Decimal number between 0 and 31

So, if we require a carriage return, we find (by looking in a table of ASCII character codes, as in Appendix I) that CR is 0D hexadecimal, or 13 decimal. Thus to accomplish our task we simply type in:

    Kermit-MS>set end 13

Finally, before setting any more parameters, we can review the current situation (either to check that we have configured everything all right so far, or to see what else needs to be done) by typing in the *status* command, i.e.

    Kermit-MS>status

(which can be shortened to typing in just "st" for "status"). This will display the current settings of all the parameters which can be configured using the "set" command. It will start off something like:

    HEATH-19 emulation On   Local echo Off
    Baud rate is 2400   Parity NONE

and so forth.

There are many more parameters which may or may not need to be configured
initially; these will be found by practice, experience or just by using the help
information available and some common sense!

14.4 Communicating with Kermit

We shall now turn our attention to actually using Kermit for real
communications. As stated earlier, Kermit does boast its own file transfer
protocol – this we will consider later. First, let us look at using the package as a
normal *terminal emulator*.

The Terminal Emulator

We enter the terminal emulation mode by using the *connect* command. This can
be done either when already inside the Kermit program, or from outside at the
DOS command level, i.e.

   Kermit-MS>connect   or
   A:\>kermit connect

The following will now be displayed:

   [Connecting to host, type Control-] C to return to PC]

and right at the bottom of the screen will be displayed (in inverse video) the
status line:

Esc chr: ^], Port 1, Speed: 2400, Parity: None, Echo: Rem, Type ^]? for Help

or whatever the current parameter settings are configured to.

Typing Control-] and then a question mark "?" (for Help) results in the
following being displayed at the top of the screen (again in inverse video):

   ? This message
   C Close the connection
   S Status of the connection
   B Send a break
   M Toggle mode line
   Q Quit logging
   R Resume logging
   O Send a null
   P Push to a new command parser

most of which are fairly self-explanatory. For instance, "S" for status simply
results in the usual status screen being displayed – the advantage of course is
that we do not have to quit out of the terminal emulator to check on the status

of any required parameter.

However, from now on the PC will function in the normal manner as a terminal emulator. If we are correctly connected up to another device via the RS-232 port, and we have correctly configured the baud rate, parity etc., then any characters being received from the RS-232 will be displayed on the screen, and conversely any characters typed in on the PC's keyboard will be transmitted down the RS-232.

File transfer using Kermit

The advantage that Kermit offers over many other communications packages is not in its terminal emulation abilities, but in its own file transfer utilities. Of course, it is necessary for both devices which are "talking" to each other to either be running Kermit, or to be running another communications package which offers the possibility of file transfer using the Kermit protocol. (One other such package is ProComm, from PIL Software Systems, P.O. Box 3492, Walnut Creek, California 94590-9998 U.S.A. This is also "freeware", that is, it is distributed as User-Supported Software).

However, given that a suitable system is available, Kermit offers a simple and almost foolproof method of file transfer. The file transfer commands which can be used are:

Send, Receive and *Get*

There are actually two methods which can be used. Either both machines must be running in the *interactive* mode, or the remote machine (which is the one that we are "talking" to) must be in *server* mode. Up until now, we have considered running Kermit in only the *interactive* mode. However, typing in the s e r v e r command at the command line prompt:

Kermit-MS>server

causes the message

Entering server mode

to be displayed. From now on the remote machine responds *to commands sent to it from our own, local, device.*

Interactive Method of File Transfer

We will first consider file transfer when both local and remote devices are in interactive mode. To *send* from our device, we must first have already given the remote machine the *receive* command. We then, (not suprisingly), simply type in the command:

Kermit-MS>send fred.txt

or whatever the name of the file is which we wish to send. Note that it is possible to type in, for instance, the command

    Kermit-MS>send fred.txt freddy.txt

In this case, Kermit picks up the file fred.txt to be sent, but transmits it under the name freddy.txt.

We would now see on the screen something like:

                    File name:
             Kbytes transferred:

                      Sending: In progress

         Number of packets: 0
          Number of retries: 0
                   Last error: None
               Last warning: None

with the appropriate fields filled with current information as the file transfer progresses.

Similarly, having issued a *send* command on our remote device, we can issue a *receive* command on our local device:

    Kermit-MS>receive fred.txt

This would display a similar status screen to the one above, in the case of sending:

                    File name:
             Kbytes transferred:

                    Receiving: In progress

         Number of packets: 0
          Number of retries: 0
                   Last error: None
               Last warning: None

File Transfer Using A Remote Server

We can, alternatively, set up one device as a *server*, and then issue commands to it from our local device. In this case, if the remote device is acting as a host computer, we will first have had to have established contact with it. This can be accomplished by entering into the terminal emulation part of Kermit (by using the *connect* command) and "logging on", invoking Kermit on the remote device, and then invoking the *server* command. Of course, the server command could be simply invoked directly on the remote device, if this is possible. We will then have the following message displayed at the bottom of the screen:

Entering server mode

From now on, all the file transfer operation is under the command of our local device. To *send* a file as before, we simply issue the send command — the remote server will automatically receive and save the file. To *receive* a file, we this time use the *get* command. We can either type in the GET command, followed by a filename, i.e.

    Kermit-MS>get fred.txt

or, if we issue just the GET command, the remote server prompts us for the required filenames:

    Kermit-MS>get
    Remote Source File:
    Local Destination File:

The file (or files) are thus transmitted by the remote device, and subsequently received and saved by our local device.

14.5 Summary of Kermit

You will hopefully by now have got just a taste of the Kermit communications package, and some of the flexibility and functionality of the program. Of course, there is more still to the package than described above, but this is left to be discovered by those who go on to actually use Kermit. And, with updates and ammendments that are issued with new releases of the package, you can be sure that Kermit will grow in popularity and be around for a long time to come.

CHAPTER 15

Crosstalk Communications Package

Following the chapter on the Kermit communications package, we now take a look at another one for the IBM PC family of microcomputers – Crosstalk XVI by Microstuf Inc.

15.1 Installing Crosstalk

Installing Crosstalk is easy; let us take the example of the IBM PC (or compatible), running under PC DOS. Then (assuming we are in the right directory) entering the command

```
A:\>xtalk
```

will "boot up" the execute file, xtalk.exe.

You may also have other Crosstalk associated files, such as the *help facility* – xtalk.hlp. There may well also be initial setup parameter files – these have the file extension ".xtk".

You will then be greeted by a welcome screen whilst the program is being loaded in, with an amusing phrase or thought for the day being displayed at the bottom for a few seconds. The program will then through you straight into the communications terminal emulation system. This is what will be displayed at the bottom of the screen:

```
Esc for ATtention, 1E00 to SWitch | Capture Off |
Local
```

However, the rest of the screen will be blank, and from now on the computer functions exactly like a terminal. If you are connected up (via the RS-232 interface) to a host computer, or some other machine, then characters received will be displayed here, and any characters input on the keyboard will likewise be displayed and transmitted.

Pressing the ESCape key will bring up the *command line* (again at the bottom of the screen):

    Command?

By this means commands, instead of data to be transmitted, can be input from the keyboard.

You may wonder how the essential setup parameters of the RS-232 interface – the baud rate, parity check etc. – are chosen. There has been no mention of them yet – indeed, a standard setup will have been used, which may not be correct for our purposes. All of the parameters can (if you know what to type in!) be changed from the command line. However, in order to see the current default parameters, you will have to *switch* screens. This is accomplished by pressing a chosen (unique) switch key, or combination of keys. A control key combination is usually ideal. In order to set this SWITCH KEY, the switch command should be typed in at the prompt

    Command?

i.e. we type in

    Command? switch

or just

    Command? sw

We will then be prompted to press the switch key combination – we may wish to use CONTROL A for instance (since this is unlikely to be used by the terminal emulation).

In this case, when control is returned to the terminal emulator (by pressing the RETURN KEY at the Command? prompt if necessary), you will now see:

    Esc for ATtention, ^A to SWitch | Capture Off | Local

from which you can see that the new definition for "SWITCH" has been registered.

What is the function of SWITCH? Pressing it will take us out of the terminal emulation, and displayed on the screen instead will be the setup parameters, and other status settings, which will look something like:

```
------- CROSSTALK-XVI Status Screen ------- Local

  NAme        XXXXX                    LOaded  A:STD.XTK
  NUmber --- NONE NECESSARY ---        CApture Off

----- Communications parameters ----- ---Filter settings---
SPeed 9600 PArity None DUplex  Full    DEbug      Off LFauto  Off
DAta  8     STop   1      EMulate VT-100 TAbex     Off
POrt  1                  MOde Call       INfilter Off OUtfiltr Off

---------- Key settings ---------- - SEnd control settings -
ATten  Esc              COmmand VT (^K) CWait None
SWitch SOH (^A)         BReak    End    LWait None
-------------------------------------------------------------
```

You will no doubt recognize some of these parameters and settings; some you may not. We will now be describe several of them, although for a full and detailed explanation of all of the functions, reference should be made to the associated manual for the product.

We can now, if necessary, change some of the RS-232 parameters. We may require, for instance, a different baud rate setting. You will now notice the difference between a package such as this, which is command line driven, and a package such as ASYNC, which uses menus. You may remember that in the ASYNC package, baud rate selection is made by moving a highlighted cursor with the cursor keys, until the required baud rate is selected, and then pressing the return key. Compare this with the Crosstalk package, in which selection is made by simply typing in the required value on the command line:

```
Command? speed 1200
```

would change the baud rate to 1200; alternatively, to make the selection quicker, we could type in:

```
Command? sp 1200
```

If we do not know which baud rates are available (since there is no menu of choices), we can simply type in:

```
Command? sp
```

which will result in the possible choices being displayed. Now typing in just

```
1200
```

will result in the required baud rate being set.

In the same way, *data* (number of data bits), *stop* (number of stop bits), and *parity* can be set. You will notice that in all cases, we need type in only the first two letters of the parameter, since this is enough for it to be uniquely identified.

You may remember the concept of *local* or *host* echo – whether or not the terminal is responsible for diplaying characters input on the keyboard itself (local), or whether the host machine will echo back characters received to be subsequently displayed on the VDU (host).

This parameter is sometimes controlled by a slightly different concept – that of *full* or *half duplex*. Strictly speaking, in a full duplex system, characters can be transmitted and received by both devices at the same time. In a half duplex system, the transfer can go either one way or the other (so there is just one transmitting device, and one receiving device) but not both. A natural consequence of this is that in a half duplex system, characters cannot be echoed, so the echoing must be done locally. Conversely, you would normally expect to find that characters are echoed by the host in a full duplex system.

Thus the *duplex* parameter can be set to determine whether characters are echoed by the host, or locally. As before, only the first two characters of the prompt need to be typed in; thus we could enter (to change from *full*, which is our current setting, back to *half*):

```
Command? duplex half
```

or, rather quicker, to change back to full duplex:

```
Command? du f
```

Another communications parameter which may be of interest is that of *emulate*. This you will see is set to VT-100; this is a terminal produced by the Digital Equipment Corporation, and is the one which has set the common standard for non-IBM terminals.

You may remember that, whilst terminals act the same way in displaying alphanumeric characters on the screen, they may differ in their interpretation of, for instance, cursor control commands, and *escape sequences*. However, the Crosstalk communications package is able to emulate a number of different types of terminals; this may need to be changed, depending on what sort of equipment the terminal emulator is connected to.

The Crosstalk Status Screen can be removed, and operation returned to the interactive terminal emulator, by hitting the return key at the Command? prompt. This will now return you to:

```
Esc for ATtention, ^A to SWitch | Capture Off | Local
```

at the bottom of the screen; the rest of the screen will be blank, or, if there has been any communication of data so far, the transmitted and received characters will be displayed.

15.2 File Transfer

We now come to one of the most important functions of the communications package – the *file transfer* capability. As with setting up parameters etc., the command line is used. The two commands in question for file transfer are CAPTURE (to receive a file of data and save to disk), and SEND (to transmit a file of data from disk). As before, these can be shortened to CA and SE.

Suppose we want to transmit a text file, which is already saved on a disk. We first need to return to the command line – this is done by calling for ATTENTION (by pressing the ESCAPE key), which returns us to the `Command?` prompt. Suppose, furthermore, that the file we wish to transmit (the appropriate disk having been inserted in,say , disk drive A) is called TEST1.TXT. We now simply type in

```
Command? se a:test1.txt
```

and press the execute key to initiate the transmission.

The file will thus be transmitted; the communications package uses XON/XOFF software handshaking, and the end of file marker used is the usual control Z (1A hexadecimal).

We may, conversely, wish to receive a file of text data, and save it to a file on disk. Thus, once again pressing the escape key to return to the command line, we type in:

```
Command? ca a:test2.txt
```

(supposing that we wish the file to be named test2.txt), and press the return key. The normal bottom status line will now be displayed again, but this time will look like:

```
Esc for ATtention, ^A to SWitch | Capture to
a:test2.txt | Local
```

From now on, any data received will be written to the disk file. If an end of file (EOF) marker is received – control Z (1A hexadecimal), the file will be closed; however, if the transmitting device does not do this, the file can be closed manually by first hitting the escape key (to regain the Command? prompt), and then typing in:

```
Command? ca -
```

which will close the file, and turn the capture off. Our status line will thus revert once again to:

```
Esc for ATtention, ^A to SWitch | Capture Off | Local
```

CHAPTER 16

Electronic Mail and Telecom Gold

Electronic Mail seems to be the flavour of the month (or year) at the moment. As its name implies, the service provides the facility of sending letters electronically from one user to another, as well as extra facilities of database interrogation, sending telexes or possibly even booking plane tickets. There are a number of services in the United Kingdom which provide a nationwide system, most notably *Easylink, One to One,* and *Telecom Gold.* The Telecom Gold service is provided by British Telecom, and at the moment boasts the largest number of subscribers in the country. We shall describe the Telecom Gold service here in some detail, both as a particular example of one system, and also as a general example of what is offered by electronic mail.

British Telecom's Telecom Gold electronic mail service uses a number of mainframe computers on which to run the service; however, users need know nothing of these, as operation appears quite independently of them. The key to the electronic mail system is that every user has a unique *mailbox* – this is used to receive and store "mail" from other users, and allow the user to read, and reply to, received mail, and also of course initiate the sending of mail to other users.

Access is gained to Telecom Gold's computers, and hence mailboxes, by means of the telephone network. Thus all a user needs to access his or her mailbox is a terminal (or terminal emulator, as described previously), and a modem (or acoustic coupler). There is no direct connection for the user to have to make to Telecom Gold's computers.

"Logging on" to the system, or "opening" a mailbox, is relatively straightforward. All you have to do is to set up your terminal (or terminal emulator) correctly, connect it to your modem or acoustic coupler, and dial through to Telecom Gold. Let us look at these points one by one.

16.1 Setting up the Terminal

The terminal configuration required will actually depend on the service which you wish to connect to, although the only difference is in the baud rate. There are three connection services offered by Telecom Gold:

    300/300 baud
    1200/75 baud
    1200/1200 baud

You will probably use either the 300/300 baud service, or the 1200/1200 service. The choice will depend only on the type of modem or acoustic coupler that you are using; less expensive ones will probably be able to cope with only a 300 baud rate, whereas a more expensive one will be able to handle 1200 baud.

Thus the baud rate should be set accordingly. The rest of the setup parameters for the RS-232 are the same for the three connection services, and are as follows:

    7 Data Bits
    1 Stop Bit
    Even Parity
    XON/XOFF (Software) Handshaking
    Host Echo (or Full Duplex, depending on the system)

Having configured your system as above, and having set the baud rate accordingly, your terminal should be ready for use.

16.2 Connecting to the Modem

You may have gathered by now, if you have read the relevant chapters on the RS-232 interface, that making up interconnecting leads to connect one device to another is by no means always straightforward. Indeed, it must be the most perplexing, and frustrating, part of communications. However, fortunately for us in this case, the backbone of the historical development of the RS-232 interface has been the problem of connecting a terminal to a modem. Thus this matter should be, hopefully, fairly simple.

The terminal will be, by definition, Data Terminal Equipment (DTE), and the modem will be, likewise by definition, Data Communications Equipment (DCE). Thus the two should connect together directly, that is, by connecting the pins together one-to-one. However, we will probably not need all of the pins connecting up; let us look at what is required.

DTE transmits on pin 2, and receives on pin 3. Conversely, DCE transmits on pin 3, and receives on pin 2. Both devices should be using pin 7 as a ground signal line. Since we will be using software handshaking (Xon/Xoff), and may thus not require any hardware handshaking signal lines, we may be able to get away with the following simple interconnection:

```
DTE (Terminal)      DCE (Modem)

            pin numbers

       2 --------------------- 2

       3 --------------------- 3

       7 --------------------- 7
```

The modem may, however, require some sort of hardware handshaking to be adhered to. If our terminal is constructed correctly, then it should deal with hardware handshake lines automatically. Remember that the DTE (terminal) will control the Request To Send (RTS–pin 4) and Data Terminal Ready (DTR–pin 20) signal lines, whereas the DCE (modem) will control the Clear To Send (CTS–pin 5), Data Set Ready (DSR–pin 6) and Data Carrier Detect (DCD–pin 8) signal lines.

Thus a more complete wiring system would be:

```
DTE (Terminal) DCE (Modem)

          pin numbers

       2 --------------------- 2

       3 --------------------- 3

       4 --------------------- 4

       5 --------------------- 5

       6 --------------------- 6

       7 --------------------- 7

       8 --------------------- 8

      20 --------------------- 20
```

Suppose, however, that the modem does require some or all relevant hardware handshake signal lines to be in the correct state, but our terminal does not set these lines as required. Since we do not require any hardware signal lines for handshaking (remember that all of the handshaking will be done in software), it is quite an easy matter for us to artificially "pull" the signal lines to the required levels.

For instance, the modem may require the DTE to pull its Request To Send signal line high, indicating that it is ready to receive data. Our terminal may not, possibly, do this (although we would normally expect it to); however, we can use the fact that the modem will, at the same time, be pulling its Clear To Send signal line high. We can thus simply connect together (on the modem side) the RTS and CTS lines, that is, pins 4 and 5. Now every time the modem goes to check to see if the DTE has pulled its RTS line high, it will think that it has actually done so. In fact, the RTS line will be high by virtue of the fact that it is the MODEM that has pulled its CTS line high.

```
DTE (Terminal)      DCE (Modem)

        pin numbers

    2 ------------------- 2

    3 ------------------- 3

    4                 ┌ 4
                      │
    5                 └ 5

    7 ------------------- 7
```

Similar trickery may be required for some or all of the other hardware handshake lines. However, with a little thought (and reference to Chapter 17) you should be able to work out such systems for yourself.

16.3 Connecting to Telecom Gold

We are now all set, with our terminal configured correctly and wired up to the modem or acoustic coupler, to connect through to the Telecom Gold service. We first have to decide which connection service we are going to use; or to put it bluntly, which telephone number we are going to dial. We have a number of choices, which fall into two categories. We can either

i) Directly dial up Telecom Gold on a London number

or

ii) Dial up a local PSE (Packet Switching Exchange) in order to connect through the PSS Network

Whilst the first option is easy and direct, it may prove expensive on telephone bills if we are dialling over a long distance. The alternative is to connect through the PSS Network – this is possible either by having a direct line into the PSS Network (but only if we are a large customer!) or by dialling up a PSE, which will hopefully be a local call to save on charges.

In either case the use of the modem, or acoustic coupler, is the same. Suppose we are using a modem. We simply dial the required number (more on that later), and wait for a whistling sound on the line. This indicates that we are through to the modem on the other end of the line. (The whistling sound is the carrier signal, used to "carry" data). Then, depending possibly on the type of modem being used, we press the DATA button of the modem. This should now connect the terminal through to the telephone line.

Note that some, more expensive, modems have a hand set built-in; this means that there will be just one connecting lead to plug into the telephone socket. However, if a separate modem and handset are being used, a split socket (to allow the modem and hand set to be plugged in at the same time) will be required.

In the case of the acoustic coupler, we dial up the required number as before. This time, when the whistling tone is heard, we simply insert the telephone receiver into the rubber cups of the acoustic coupler (making sure that they are the right way around, of course).

In either case the carrier light should come on (indicating that all is well, and that the carrier signal has been detected).

Next we need to know which telephone number we have to dial. Suppose we are dialling directly through to Telecom Gold in London. Then we have three choices, depending on the chosen baud rate (as mentioned above). The possibilities are:

   300/300 baud 01 583 3000
   1200/75 baud 01 583 1275
   1200/1200 baud 01 583 1200

(The "01" prefix is, of course, only necessary if you are dialling from outside London).

Alternatively, we may wish to go through a Packet Switching Exchange. In this case, the number we need to dial will depend on the area of the country we are in, as well as the baud rate. For instance, if we are in the Birmingham area, the numbers are as follows:

   300/300 baud 021 214 5139
   1200/75 baud 021 214 6191
   1200/1200 baud 021 214 3061

Full details of all the telephone numbers for different parts of the country are provided by Telecom Gold.

We must now perform a "log on" routine, to connect through to the required computer, and get into our mailbox. This differs slightly between phoning direct, and phoning a local PSE.

Phoning Direct

When the carrier light has turned on, we simply press the return key twice. If all is well and we are connected through correctly, we should see displayed on our screen an opening message from Telecom Gold, and the PAD' prompt, like this:

```
Telecom Gold Network:
This is Pad 081 line 4 speed 1200
PAD>
```

We now have to "call" up the computer system that our mailbox is on (we will have been advised this when receiving the mailbox from Telecom Gold). For instance, we may be on computer number 83. In this case we type in:

```
PAD>call 83
```

and press return. We will now see the following:

```
Primecom Network 18.4A System 81

Please sign on
>
```

We are almost there! All we have to do is to enter in our identity number, and our own password (which we can set, and change when we like). Our identity number may be, for instance, ABC999, and our password PASS. (The password will not be displayed on the screen when we type it in, so that it will not be revealed to onlookers). Thus we would see:

```
>ID ABC999
Password?
   (enter ''PASS'' and press return)
```

If the ID and the password are correct, we will be connected through to our mailbox.

Phoning a PSE

In this case, we have to first press the return key twice, and then enter either A2, or D1, and then press the return key again. If we are connected through all right to the PSS, we will be asked to enter our NETWORK USER IDENTIFICATION:

```
NUI?
```

We thus have to type in Telecom Gold's NUI (or our own, if we have one). In the case of Telecom Gold we would have to enter:

```
NTLGOLD901TYM
```

and then press return.

The system now replies:

```
ADD?
```

as it requires the NETWORK USER ADDRESS (NUA) of Telecom Gold to be entered, followed by the number of the computer in which our mailbox resides. So we would have to enter, if our mailbox is in, say, computer number 83:

```
A21920100483
```

There will now be a response to indicate that we are through to the system in London. We then enter our identification and password as before.

Having logged on to our mailbox successfully, we will be greeted by a message similar to the following:

```
TELECOM GOLD Automated Office Services 18.3A(83)
On At 18.54 11/3/86
Last On At 12.22 12/1/86

Mail call (1 Unread,1 Unread Express,Total 2)

>
```

You will see that we are told the current time and date of logging on, and also the last time we were logged into the system. There is also information about our mailbox — we may have received some "letters" since we last logged on, which we have not yet read.

Although an exhaustive account of Telecom Gold's features is not possible in this chapter (for that you should refer to Telecom Gold's own manuals), an outline of some of the services will be given to illustrate the sort of product that is on offer.

The Mail Service

As you might expect by now, it is possible to "send" the electronic equivalent of "letters" to other users, and also to receive and read them. Indeed the electronic mail facilities of Telecom Gold become much more extensive than this, as it is possible to send copies of the same "electronic letter" to a number of people at the same time, send "carbon copies", and even request an acknowledgement or reply to your letter. To enter the mail service you simply have to, quite appropriately, type in "MAIL" at the cursor prompt, thus:

```
>mail
```

whereupon the response will come back:

```
Send, Read or Scan?
```

These are the three basic options of the mail service. SEND and READ are self-explanatory; SCAN is a convenient type of reading which means only the header of a received letter has to be looked at, and not the body of it.

Let us look at these three functions one by one.

Sending Mail

Typing in "SEND" after the query

```
Send, Read or Scan?
```

will next prompt for:

```
To:
```

Obviously we now have to type in the person (or people) we wish to send the letter to. How is this to be specified? There are actually a number of ways in which this can be done, some of which are more "friendly" than others.

For instance, you will remember from logging on to the system that you had to type in your identification – which is your name to the system. For instance you may have the ID, as in the example above, of ABC999. In fact, in full this is prefixed by the number of the computer in which your mailbox presides, i.e. your name is 83:ABC999. Thus, you may similarly specify someone else on the system; for instance, someone with a mailbox on the same computer as you may have the ID of EFG111, whilst somebody else on another system may have the ID of, say, 79:HIJ222.

However, there is a neater way of specifying a name, which is more friendly to us mortal beings. For it is possible to set up lists of names, or directories, setting computer identification numbers against more commonly used names. For instance, you may construct a list as follows:

```
A.SMITH     EFG111    ALISON
P.SIMONS    79:HIJ222    PETE
```

We could thus reply to the TO: prompt by:
```
EFG111 79:HIJ222
```

or by, say:
```
ALISON PETE
```

or a combination of the above. Thus, sending items becomes more straightforward — it is not always necessary to have to remember a person's identification number, as it may be possible to use just, say, their christian name.

Having entered the required list of names that you want a copy of the letter to be sent to, you will be prompted:

```
Subject:
```

You can thus give the letter a title, to specify its contents and give some indication to the receiver what the letter is about (remember that this subject header is what will be seen when Scanning).

Having entered a subject description, you will next be prompted to enter the main body of the letter as follows:

```
Text:
```

It is now a simple case of typing in whatever you need, as with a normal wordprocessor package (if you should happen to have used one). Once you have entered everything that you want to, you will of course be wishing to actually send the letter. This is accomplished by typing in ".S" — one of the available "dot commands". Having done this, acknowledgement will be given that the letter or letters have been sent to the required mailboxes, and the cursor prompt will once again be displayed.

Of course you may decide half way through the letter that you do not, after all, want to proceed with it. In this case it is possible to "quit" out of the system by typing in another "dot command", this time ".Q".

There are, as you might by now expect, numerous other commands and dot commands that can be invoked; these you will surely discover should you ever use the system.

Reading Mail

You will remember that after typing in the 'MAIL prompt, you are presented
with the options

    Send, Read or Scan?

Typing in READ (or just R for short will do), will mean that any received mail
will be displayed. For instance, the first letter received might be as follows:

    To: F.Freddy (ABC999)
    From: A.Smith (DEF111)

    Posted:Wed 19-Oct-86 9:30 Sys 83(4)

    Subject:Dummy Letter

    -More-

You will notice that the system tells you who sent the letter, the time and day on
which it was sent, and the subject header of the letter. If you now wish to read
the letter, you simply have to press the return key. Now the whole text of the
letter will be displayed to you.

Alternatively, you may not be interested in reading the contents of the letter. In
this case it is possible to skip onto the next received letter (if there is one), by
typing in NEXT. However, if you have decided to read the text, then when it has
all been displayed the following prompt will be displayed:

    Action required:

There are now a number of options for you to choose from. (The responses are
indicated by the words in capital letters). You may wish to REPLY to the person
who sent you the letter (thus bypassing the procedure of having to specify
explicitly their user identification or name). Or you may wish to read the letter
again. Alternatively, you may wish to FOrward the letter (followed by a name),
along with comments, to someone else to read as well. Other options include
DEL to delete the message, QUIT to go back to the ">" prompt, or HELP if
you are stuck!

Scanning Mail

You may think that it would be rather tedious to have to plough your way
through your mail to see what you have received, although as you may have
noticed it is not necessary to have to read the body of the mail every time.
However, there is a slightly quicker way of seeing what other people have sent
you—*scanning* the mail. This is, as you would by now expect, accessed by typing
in SCAN at the prompt

You will now be shown a list of all received messages in your mailbox. The list starts at the "top" of the mailbox (and will additionally start with any messages received by "Express" mail—a priority mailing service), and will tell you who sent the message, when the message was sent, the system from which the message was sent, the subject header of the message, and also (most usefully) the number of lines of text in the message.

Having scanned your mail you may, of course, then selectively read any messages which interest you. Note that there is an even faster scanning method, called *quickscan* (which is accessed by typing in "QSC"), which condenses the information even further.

Other Features of Telecom Gold

An Electronic Mail service such as Telecom Gold is certainly most useful as far as the features already described go. However, there is more. The Telecom Gold service is part of the international Dialcom system, so it is possible to send messages to a user in, say, the United States, or any other country with a similar Dialcom service. In fact, there is no difference between sending a message to someone in Manchester or Miami; your Miami friend will just be on a different computer system, and will thus have a different system number (say, 52). Thus for Manchester you would simply have to type in (at the "To:" prompt), for example, 83:ABC123, whilst for Miami it might be perhaps 52:DEF456. Easy, isn't it?

There are many other features, which would be discovered and learnt on using the service extensively. For instance, messages may be prepared off-line, and then (at some later date, perhaps), sent as mail. This is particularly useful for another feature—sending a TELEX. Of course, telexes can also be received into your mailbox. Additionally, there are noticeboards to read for information, a system for having a "chat", and even games to play!

All in all, electronic mail services such as Telecom Gold offer useful and flexible modern alternatives to the paper letter and telephone. Whilst certainly not supplanting more traditional methods of communication (at least, not for the time being), they do certainly have many advantages. Perhaps their two biggest drawbacks, at least in this country, are the relatively high cost of using the telephone network, and the slow baud rates that have to be used for data communication between terminal and host computer via modems. For whilst the majority of users in the U.K. probably content themselves with using 300 baud services (with 1200 baud an absolute maximum), users in the U.S.A. are already enjoying 2400 baud services.

CHAPTER 17

RS-232 Wiring Connections in the Real World

Introduction

We now come to the nitty gritty of living with the RS-232 interface—how to connect two devices—which could be anything, from any manufacturer (reputable or not!)—without giving up in horror at the whole process. Unfortunately, not all models of personal computers, printers, modems and the like can be considered here; only some of the more popular ones. However, if your particular combination is not included, there will hopefully be enough information for you to have some hope of success in your venture.

17.1 Initial Considerations

Before embarking on the task in hand, it is wise first to try to convince yourself that what you are trying to achieve is in fact not only highly possible, but also (once done) probably very easy as well! What are the first steps we need to take?

First of all, it will be necessary to look at the kind of connectors used by the two machines in question. This is not a trivial point, for whilst most RS-232 interfaces will use a 25 pin D-type connector, as previously described, not all will do so. Notably, the combined serial/parallel card which IBM PCs and compatibles use has (rather confusingly) a 25 pin D-type for the *parallel* printer port, and a 9 pin D-type connector for the RS-232. However, you may find PC's with a single RS-232 card, using a 25 pin D-type only. Also, the Acorn BBC series do not use D-type connectors at all, but 5 pin DIN-type round sockets. Also, the Apple Macintosh uses a 9 pin D-type.

Next, you will need to determine whether the devices are configured as **DTE** (Data Terminal Equipment) or **DCE** (Data Communications Equipment). Remember what this means. If we consider just the transmit and receive lines for a moment, then, according to the RS-232 standards, Data Terminal Equipment uses pin 2 for transmitting , and pin 3 for receiving (if a standard 25 pin D-type is being used), whilst Data Communications Equipment does it the other way round—pin 2 is used for receiving, and pin 3 for transmitting. Note, however, that rather confusing terminology is used, for pin 2 is *always* referred to as TxD, and pin 3 is likewise always referred to as RxD (notwithstanding the fact that TxD might be the receive line, and RxD the transmit line!)

Another purely practical consideration – when obtaining the parts necessary to complete the job – is the gender of the connectors to be used. There is no strict rule for determining beforehand what is required, so you will have to study the machines in question.

Finally, do not forget to have an adequate supply of suitable cable!

17.2 How Many Lines Will Need to be Connected?

It will be worthwhile spending a little time before jumping into the deep end to consider what the *minimum* number of connnecting wires should be. At the very least, it may be just two! In practice, however, you will find quite often that it is only three. For if there is no hardware handshaking to be done, then this is all that we will require:

    1 transmit line
    1 receive line
    1 signal ground line

However, we may find that we are unable to ignore some or all of the hardware handshake lines. We now have a further consideration – are these lines to be used for actual handshaking, or just to keep a temperamental device happy? For instance, if we have configured our system to use hardware handshaking to control the flow of data (e.g. RTS/CTS), then we will obviously have to connect these two lines together too. Thus we now require *five* lines:

    1 transmit line
    1 receive line
    1 signal ground line
    1 RTS line
    1 CTS line

On the other hand, we may be using software handshaking (e.g. XON/XOFF), but with a machine which nevertheless requires one or more of its hardware handshake signal lines to be in the correct state before it will do anything. For instance, we may be connected to a terminal which will not "talk" to us until it sees the Data Set Ready (DSR) line go "high". It will be seen that there are two ways to handle this problem, which will depend partly on the way in which the second device controls its hardware handshake signal lines. If the DCE *does* automatically pull its DSR line "high", then we could connect up this line as well. However, this is more likely not to be the case, and anyway, we may wish to keep the number of interconnecting lines to a minimum. There is, however, an alternative solution. For if the terminal we are connecting to requires the DSR line to be set **high,** then it should in turn (if it is sticking to the RS-232 standard) be setting its Data Terminal Ready (DTR) line **high**. We can then use a common trick of simply connecting together – *at the terminal end* – the DSR and DTR signal pins. This will have the desired effect – for when the terminal is ready, it will check the DSR line. However, it will have set its DTR line **high** – and will thus see the DSR line as **high** as well!

Finally, there may be no alternative but to connect together all – or almost all – of the RS-232's possible 25 lines. This will be either because we find that a lot of the hardware handshake lines are actually used, or because we may be making up a general purpose lead which we need to work under a variety of circumstances and with a number of devices.

Let us now consider some examples.

17.3 Wiring Examples

Before considering some real-life examples of devices to connect together, it will be instructive first to connect together some theoretical ones (manufacturers' ranges of machines change quite frequently – theoretical ones do not!)

DTE to DCE – No Hardware Handshaking

This is perhaps the easiest of the lot, and will actually be the solution in many real examples. To cater for both transmitting and receiving, we need to connect from DTE's transmit line (pin 2) to DCE's receive line (also pin 2), and from DTE's receive line (pin 3) to DCE's receive line (also pin 3). Finally, we need to connect the two signal ground pins together (both of which use pin 7).

```
                    DTE                      DCE

TxD                  2 ---------------------- 2

RxD                  3 ---------------------- 3

Gnd                  7 ---------------------- 7
```

Fig. 17.1

DTE to DCE—With RTS/CTS Hardware Handshaking

Suppose we now require full RTS/CTS hardware handshaking. What is now required? This, fortunately, is again quite straightforward. We just connect pin 4 to pin 4 (RTS signal line) and pin 5 to pin 5 (CTS line).

```
                    DTE                   DCE

TxD                  2 --------------------- 2

RxD                  3 --------------------- 3

RTS                  4 --------------------- 4

CTS                  5 --------------------- 5

Gnd                  7 --------------------- 7
```

Fig. 17.2

DTE to DCE—With RTS/CTS and DSR/DTR Hardware Handshaking

We may also find on occasions that we need to cater for the Data Set Ready and Data Terminal Ready lines. This is a simple extension:

```
                    DTE                   DCE

TxD                  2 --------------------- 2

RxD                  3 --------------------- 3

RTS                  4 --------------------- 4

CTS                  5 --------------------- 5

DSR                  6 --------------------- 6

Gnd                  7 --------------------- 7

DTR                 20 --------------------- 20
```

Fig. 17.3

However, it is quite probable in this case that we are overdoing things! For it is likely that only the RTS and CTS lines will be used for actual handshaking—it is just that the DTE requires the DSR line to be pulled high. So, as we described in Section 17.2, we can cheat at the terminal's end:

```
              DTE              DCE

TxD            2 ------------------- 2

RxD            3 ------------------- 3

RTS            4 ------------------- 4

CTS            5 ------------------- 5

Gnd            7 ------------------- 7

DSR            6 ─┐
DTR           20 ─┘
```

Fig. 17.4

Catering for Data Carrier Detect as well

Finally, we may on rare occasions find that the DTE is paying some attention to
the DCE's Data Carrier Detect (DCD or just CD) signal line. In this case we
could try connecting it straight through, if we know that the DCE is going to do
something reasonable with it:

```
              DTE              DCE

TxD            2 ------------------- 2

RxD            3 ------------------- 3

RTS            4 ------------------- 4

CTS            5 ------------------- 5

Gnd            7 ------------------- 7

DCD            8 ------------------- 8

DSR            6 ─┐
DTR           20 ─┘
```

Fig. 17.5

However, it is more than likely that we are stuck with a fussy DTE which requires
DCD to be pulled **high**, and a DCE which does not care to control this line at
all. In this case, we can just extend our "cheating" with the wiring at the DTE
end, and connect pin 8 to pins 6 and 20, which are already connected together:

185

                    DTE   DCE

TxD   2 ------------------- 2

RxD   3 ------------------- 3

RTS   4 ------------------- 4

CTS   5 ------------------- 5

Gnd   7 ------------------- 7

DSR   6 ┐
DCD   8 ┤
DTR   20 ┘

Fig. 17.6

Wiring DTE to DTE (or DCE to DCE)

In all the above cases we have been wiring DTE to DCE. However, this may well
not be the case. We may wish to wire together, for instance, two microcomputers
in order to transfer ("dump") a file of data from one to the other. It is most likely
that the two devices will both be wired as DTE.

The solution is, of course, most simple. On the one hand, one DTE will be using
pin 2 for transmitting and pin 3 for receiving, whilst the other DTE will be doing
the same as well. So we just have to cross the transmit and receive wires over:

                    DTE   DTE

TxD   2 ------------------- 3

RxD   3 ------------------- 2

Gnd   7 ------------------- 7

Fig. 17.7

Similarly, if we require **hardware handshaking** using the RTS and CTS signal
lines as well, we just cross over the corresponding pair of lines:

	DTE		DTE
TxD	2	----------------------	3
RxD	3	----------------------	2
RTS	4	----------------------	5
CTS	5	----------------------	4
Gnd	7	----------------------	7

Fig. 17.8

Finally, we may also need to do the same trick with the DSR/DTR signal line pair:

	DTE		DTE
TxD	2	----------------------	3
RxD	3	----------------------	2
RTS	4	----------------------	5
CTS	5	----------------------	4
DSR	6	----------------------	20
DTR	20	----------------------	6
Gnd	7	----------------------	7

Fig. 17.9

We would usually find we could just employ our "trick" with the DSR and DTR lines at *both* ends this time:

	DTE		DTE
TxD	2	----------------------	3
RxD	3	----------------------	2
RTS	4	----------------------	5
CTS	5	----------------------	4
Gnd	7	----------------------	7
DSR	6 ┐		┌ 6
DCD	8 ┤		├ 8
DTR	20 ┘		└ 20

Fig. 17.10

Final Theoretical Example

In almost all cases that you will come across, with devices that use the RS-232 lines in a standard way, you will find that one of the above examples will fit the bill.

Let us finally consider one more example (which, although here referred to as a theoretical one, did actually once occur in practice). Suppose we have the task of connecting a DCE to a DTE. Suppose, furthermore, that we are using some sort of software handshaking (which in this case was not XON/XOFF, but that is an irrelevance). However, suppose that our DCE does not have any capability of controlling any of the hardware handshake signal lines (CTS, DSR and DCD), but our DTE requires the CTS and DSR signal lines to be in the correct state before it will do anything. What are we to do?

You may well find that in some tricky situations like this the only solution is to use a tool like a *line tester* and *patch box*, or a combination of the two called a *breakout box*. A line tester is a simple device which consists of a box with a 25 pin D-type on either end, and some LEDs (Light Emitting Diodes) on the top. There will be one LED connected to each of the most important RS-232 lines—TxD, RxD, RTS, CTS,DSR, DTR and possibly DCD. The LEDs will operate in the following sort of way: when a *positive* voltage is present on the signal line, they will glow in one colour (e.g. green), and when a *negative* voltage is present, they will glow in another colour (e.g. red). If the signal line is at a zero potential, they will not glow at all. Thus, by plugging the breakout box in between the two devices in question, it will be possible to see at any time both the state of the signal lines, and also (by observing any fleeting flickering on the transmit and receive lines) whether any data is being transferred.

We may find a device such as a *patch box* useful for experimenting with different cross-connections in the RS-232 interfacing lead. As its name implies, the box enables us to patch, using temporary connecting leads, from pins on one side of the interface to any other pin (or pins) on the other side. This certainly saves a lot of time in soldering and desoldering connections!

We will probably have discovered the information about the hardware handshaking characteristics of the device in question ourselves; we will be very lucky indeed to find all such detailed information in a reference manual (if such a manual exists!).

By connecting the breakout box in place, we can now see what happens when the device we are connecting to is turned on. We know (or suspect) already that the device will require the DCE's CTS and DSR signal lines to go **high** correctly. We would thus expect it to be well behaved all round—indeed it is, as we notice that, on turning on, the DTE pulls its *DTR* signal line **high**. Now, remembering

our previous trick of connecting one signal line which we know to be pulled high
to another, which we require to be pulled high, we can extend this idea one stage
further – by connecting the DTR line from the DTE to both the CTS *and* the
DSR pins *at the DTE end of the connection.*

```
                      DTE                    DCE

TxD                    2 ---------------------- 2

RxD                    3 ---------------------- 3

Gnd                    7 ---------------------- 7

CTS                    5 ─┐
                          │
DSR                    6 ─┤
                          │
DTR                   20 ─┘
```

Fig. 17.11

Now everything should work! Note, however, that the DTE's RTS signal line is
left untouched – although the DTE will certainly be "toggling" it up and down
as it starts and stops transmitting and receiving characters (which we will be able
to see by observing the corresponding LED of the break out box flashing
between green and red).

17.4 Some Actual Machines

Let us now consider how to wire up the RS-232 interfaces of some actual
production machines (most of which are still available, although some are
included as old favourites, as they may still be found in everyday use).

Again, since there are so many different machines on the market, with so many
different interfaces, it is not possible to show every possible combination. This
will not even be attempted with the selected list of devices below! Instead, we
will consider connecting an "ideal" machine (i.e. one which behaves well, as far
as controlling its RS-232 interface goes), to each of the "real" machines. Thus,
armed with the knowledge of how a machine performs in reality, it should be
possible to connect together two devices (which are perhaps *both* not so well-
behaved) with some degree of success.

IBM PC (25 pin D-type Connector) and Compatibles

We first come to one of the most popular and widespread configurations
around – the IBM PC with all its cohorts of look-alikes and compatibles.
Fortunately the RS-232 interface is reasonably well-behaved, although with a
reliance on having the hardware signal lines in the correct state.

The first consideration is whether to use hardware or software handshaking. Personally, I always prefer to use software handshaking (just simple XON/XOFF, or a more sophisticated file transfer protocol such as XMODEM or KERMIT)—although this may not always be possible. Most of the commercially-available communications packages will offer software handshaking; however, problems may arise when accessing the RS-232 port directly from PC-DOS, or the BASIC programming language. In both cases, it will benecessary to use *hardware (RTS/CTS) handshaking*.

General Purpose Interface for the IBM

```
IBM                    (DTE)                   DCE

TxD                      2 --------------------- 2

RxD                      3 --------------------- 3

RTS                      4 --------------------- 4

CTS                      5 --------------------- 5

Gnd                      7 --------------------- 7

DSR                      6 ┐
DTR                     20 ┘
```

Fig. 17.12

Notice that the old trick of connecting the DSR and DTR pins together at the IBM end—when the IBM pulls DTR **high**, it will see the DSR signal line go high as well. Note also one practical point when constructing a lead—the RS-232 connector on the IBM tends to be a *plug* (i.e. male connector).

IBM AT (9 pin D-type Connector) and Compatibles

Another option for the communications card for an IBM is a combined serial-parallel board. This incorporates both a Centronics parallel port (using a 25-pin D-type connector), and an RS-232 port (using a 9-pin D-type connector). These are the pin connections for the RS-232:

Pin number	Description	From IBM	To IBM
1	Carrier Detect (DCD)		X
2	Receive Data (RxD)		X
3	Transmit Data (TxD)	X	
4	Data Terminal Ready (DTR)	X	
5	Signal Ground		
6	Data Set Ready (DSR)		X
7	Request To Send (RTS)	X	
8	Clear To Send (CTS)		X
9	Ring Indicator		X

Fig. 17.13

Thus our general purpose connection will be as follows:

```
              IBM  (DTE)              DCE
              9 pin  D-type     25 pin D-type

TxD             3 --------------------- 2

RxD             2 --------------------- 3

RTS             7 --------------------- 4

CTS             8 --------------------- 5

Gnd             5 --------------------- 7

DSR             6 ┐
                  │
DTR             4 ┘
```

Fig. 17.14

Note that the 9 pin D-type connector on the IBM board is a *plug* (i.e. a male connector).

ACT Apricot

The Apricot series of microcomputers, running the MS-DOS operating system and using 3½ inch disks instead of the IBM standard of 5¼ inch ones, has proven most popular in the United Kingdom and is the backbone of many installations. However, the range has now been all but discontinued by Apricot (formerly ACT) in favour of the Xen range of IBM PC compatibles.

The RS-232 is, thankfully, most well behaved. The machine was supplied with a 25 pin D-type connector as standard – however, note that a female *socket* is used on the back of the machine, instead of IBM's male plug.

The Apricot is wired as DTE. Also, earlier versions of the machine had a very good communications package bundled in with the machine, called *Async*. This communications package is a general purpose terminal emulator, and also has (ASCII text) file transfer capability.The package has the choice of selecting between software handshaking (XON/XOFF) or having none at all – thus, in practice, there will probably be little need to use anything other than software handshaking. The wiring configuration for the RS-232 is further simplified by the fact that the Apricot does not require its hardware handshake signal lines to be in any particular state for communication. Thus, the following is all that is required to communicate with a device which, in turn, is using no more than software handshaking:

```
                Apricot (DTE)                DCE
                25 pin D-type

TxD                 2 ---------------------- 2

RxD                 3 ---------------------- 3

Gnd                 7 ---------------------- 7
```

Fig. 17.15

BBC B and Master Series

The BBC series of microcomputers – designed and manufactured by Acorn, which is now part of Olivetti – is very popular because the BBC specified the design and recommended the computer to be used in schools and colleges for educational courses. However, the RS-232 supplied as standard with the machine is unusual in two respects. First, it is strictly not an RS-232, but rather an RS-423 (as described previously). In practice this means that a 5V signal level is used instead of the recommended 12V; remember though, that the RS-232 specification allows the voltage present on the signal lines to be in the range from 3V–12V, so the RS-423 is actually compatible. Secondly, the standard 25 pin D-type connector is not used. The connector is not even a 9 pin D-type! Rather, a 5 pin DIN round socket is used (similar to connectors used in some Hi-Fi systems). Unfortunately, the pin arrangement is symmetrical, so determining the wiring is not usually very straightforward.

The BBC utilises just five lines – transmit, receive, two hardware handshake lines and a signal ground. Whether or not we need to wire up the RTS and CTS signal lines will depend on how we are communicating (i.e. if it is from a BBC basic program, or communications package). The following wiring will cover all cases:

```
          BBC                      DCE

      Data  Out --------------------- 2

      Data  In ---------------------- 3

      RTS         --------------------- 4

      CTS         --------------------- 5

      Gnd         --------------------- 7
```

Fig. 17.16

Amstrad 4 and 6 Series

The still popular 8-bit (Zilog Z80) range of home and small office computers (i.e. the CPC464, CPC6128, and the 8256 and 8512) from Amstrad do not come with an RS-232 serial interface as standard; however,this can be purchased as a separate item, which connects via the expansion port on the machine. Despite the domination of the 16-bit MS-DOS machines, the success of the Amstrad has meant a resurgence of interest in the CP/M operating system.

This is the pin configuration of the RS-232 interface for the CPC464 and CPC6128 as supplied by Amstrad themselves, although other manufacturers do also produce their own versions. Note that a standard 25 pin D-type male plug is used:

Pin number	Description	From Amstrad	To Amstrad
2	Transmit Data (TxD)	X	
3	Receive Data (RxD)		X
4	Request To Send (RTS)	X	
5	Clear To Send (CTS)		X
7	Signal Ground		
8	Carrier Detect (DCD)		X
20	Data Terminal Ready (DTR)	X	
22	Ring Indicator		X

Fig. 17.17

Note that pin 6, which is normally assigned to Data Set Ready (DSR),is not used.

The interface is supplied with a manual (called the "Book of Spells"!) outlining the functioning of the interface, and how to utilize it. Again, consideration has to be given to the method by which communication is taking place, as the wiring will greatly vary depending on this. For instance,the simplest method is to use CP/M, set up with Xon/Xoff software handshaking. (CP/M Version 2.2 has a *Setup* command, whilst CP/M Plus uses the *Setsio* function). Thus, for instance in CP/M Plus, the RS-232 port can be configured to 4800 baud, eight data bits, no parity, and Xon/Xoff handshaking by the following command:

```
A>setsio 4800 bits 8 par none hand off x on
```

then a file transfer from the Amstrad to another device can be accomplished by using the **PIP** (Peripheral Interface Program) command:

```
A>pip aux:=fred.txt
```

or from an external device to the Amstrad by:

```
A>pip fred1.txt=aux:
```

Thus, all that is required is the wiring example as in Fig. 17.15.

However, if CP/M is not being used, but rather one of the calls through AMSDOS (the Amstrad Operating System), then hardware handshaking will have to be used instead. (There are file transfer commands which can be used, such as "|INFILE" and "|OUTFILE"). Unfortunately, the hardware handshaking used is not quite straightforward. When transmitting from the Amstrad to another device, normal RTS/CTS handshaking is used. However, when the Amstrad is receiving, it expects the Data Carrier Detect (DCD) from the DCE to be doing the handshaking, and will respond with its Data Terminal Ready signal line. Thus we have, effectively, DCD/DTR handshaking.

So a full wiring configuration would be:

```
        Amstrad       (DTE)                    DCE
TxD                     2 --------------------- 2
RxD                     3 --------------------- 3
RTS                     4 --------------------- 4
CTS                     5 --------------------- 5
Gnd                     7 --------------------- 7
DCD                     8 --------------------- 8
DTR                    20 --------------------- 20
```

Fig. 17.18

However, we may have a DCE which does not control its DCD signal lineas required (this is most likely). In this case, we will have to use the DCE's CTS line instead. Thus, for sending *to* the Amstrad only, the following is necessary:

```
        Amstrad        (DTE)               DCE

TxD            2 ---------------------- 2

RxD            3 ---------------------- 3

Gnd            7 ---------------------- 7

DCD            8 ---------------------- 5

DTR           20 ---------------------- 4
```

Fig. 17.19

Apple Macintosh

The Macintosh, from Apple Corporation, uses a 9 pin D-type connector for its RS-232 connection. In fact, there are two provided as standard, one as a modem port and the other as a printer port. Which one is used will depend on the configuration of the device – for instance, when using Apple's own MacTerminal (a terminal emulation program, of course), as well as determining baud rate, parity and the like, the RS-232 port being used can be selected.

The following wiring will suffice when connecting to a DCE. Note that only the CTS signal line is wired up; we are assuming that MacTerminal is set to Xon/Xoff handshaking. However, the Macintosh may need to see that the CTS line is high.

```
        Macintosh (DTE)              DCE
          9 pin D-type

TxD            5 ---------------------- 2

RxD            7 ---------------------- 3

Gnd            3 ---------------------- 7

CTS            9 ---------------------- 5
```

Fig. 17.20

APPENDIX I

The ASCII Character Set

Decimal	Hexadecimal	ASCII	Control Code
0	00	NUL	<CTRL>@
1	01	SOH	<CTRL>A
2	02	STX	<CTRL>B
3	03	ETX	<CTRL>C
4	04	EOT	<CTRL>D
5	05	ENQ	<CTRL>E
6	06	ACK	<CTRL>F
7	07	BEL	<CTRL>G
8	08	BS	<CTRL>H
9	09	HT	<CTRL>I
10	0A	LF	<CTRL>J
11	0B	VT	<CTRL>K
12	0C	FF	<CTRL>L
13	0D	CR	<CTRL>M
14	0E	SO	<CTRL>N
15	0F	SI	<CTRL>O
16	10	DLE	<CTRL>P
17	11	DC1	<CTRL>Q
18	12	DC2	<CTRL>R
19	13	DC3	<CTRL>S
20	14	DC4	<CTRL>T
21	15	NAK	<CTRL>U
22	16	SYN	<CTRL>V
23	17	ETB	<CTRL>W
24	18	CAN	<CTRL>X
25	19	EM	<CTRL>Y
26	1A	SUB	<CTRL>Z
27	1B	ESC	
28	1C	FS	
29	1D	GS	
30	1E	RS	
31	1F	US	
32	20	SP	
33	21	!	
34	22	”	

35	23	£
36	24	$
37	25	%
38	26	&
39	27	'
40	28	(
41	29	)
42	2A	*
43	2B	+
44	2C	,
45	2D	−
46	2E	.
47	2F	/
48	30	0
49	31	1
50	32	2
51	33	3
52	34	4
53	35	5
54	36	6
55	37	7
56	38	8
57	39	9
58	3A	:
59	3B	;
60	3C	<
61	3D	=
62	3E	>
63	3F	?
64	40	@
65	41	A
66	42	B
67	43	C
68	44	D
69	45	E
70	46	F
71	47	G
72	48	H
73	49	I
74	4A	J
75	4B	K
76	4C	L
77	4D	M
78	4E	N
79	4F	O

80	50	P
81	51	Q
82	52	R
83	53	S
84	54	T
85	55	U
86	56	V
87	57	W
88	58	X
89	59	Y
90	5A	Z
91	5B	[
92	5C	\
93	5D	]
94	5E	
95	5F	
96	60	___
97	61	a
98	62	b
99	63	c
100	64	d
101	65	e
102	66	f
103	67	g
104	68	h
105	69	i
106	6A	j
107	6B	k
108	6C	l
109	6D	m
110	6E	n
111	6F	o
112	70	p
113	71	q
114	72	r
115	73	s
116	74	t
117	75	u
118	76	v
119	77	w
120	78	x
121	79	y
122	7A	z
123	7B	{
124	7C		

125	7D	}
126	7E	
127	7F	DEL

The Control Code Symbols

NUL	Null
SOH	Start of Heading
STX	Start of Text
ETX	End of Text
EOT	End of Transmission
ENQ	Enquiry
ACK	Acknowledge
BEL	Bell
BS	Backspace
HT	Horizontal Tabulation
LF	Line Feed
VT	Vertical Tabulation
FF	Form Feed
CR	Carriage Return
SO	Shift Out
SI	Shift In
DLE	Data Link Escape
DC	Device Control
NAK	Negative Acknowledge
SYN	Synchronous Idle
ETB	End of Transmission Block
CAN	Cancel
EM	End of Medium
SUB	Substitute
ESC	Escape
FS	File Separator
GS	Group Separator
RS	Record Separator
US	Unit Separator
SP	Space
DEL	Delete

The EBCDIC Character Set

Decimal	*Hexadecimal*	*EBCDIC*
0	00	NUL
1	01	SOH
2	02	STX
3	03	ETX
4	04	SEL
5	05	HT
6	06	RNL
7	07	DEL
8	08	GE
9	09	SPS
10	0A	RPT
11	0B	VT
12	0C	FF
13	0D	CR
14	0E	SO
15	0F	SI
16	10	DLE
17	11	DC1
18	12	DC2
19	13	DC3
20	14	RES/ENP
21	15	NL
22	16	BS
23	17	POC
24	18	CAN
25	19	EM
26	1A	UBS
27	1B	CU1
28	1C	IFS
29	1D	IGS
30	1E	IRS
31	1F	ITB/IUS

32	20	DS
33	21	SOS
34	22	FS
35	23	WUS
36	24	BYP/INP
37	25	LF
38	26	ETB
39	27	ESC
40	28	SA
41	29	SFE
42	2A	SM/SW
43	2B	CSP
44	2C	MFA
45	2D	ENQ
46	2E	ACK
47	2F	BEL
48	30	
49	31	
50	32	SYN
51	33	IR
52	34	PP
53	35	TRN
54	36	NBS
55	37	EOT
56	38	SBS
57	39	IT
58	3A	RFF
59	3B	CU3
60	3C	DC4
61	3D	NAK
62	3E	
63	3F	SUB
64	40	Sp
65	41	
66	42	
67	43	
68	44	
69	45	
70	46	
71	47	
72	48	
73	49	
74	4A	
75	4B	
76	4C	<

77	4D	(
78	4E	+
79	4F	
80	50	&
81	51	
82	52	
83	53	
84	54	
85	55	
86	56	
87	57	
88	58	
89	59	
90	5A	!
91	5B	$
92	5C	*
93	5D	)
94	5E	;
95	5F	
96	60	−
97	61	/
98	62	
99	63	
100	64	
101	65	
102	66	
103	67	
104	68	
105	69	
106	6A	|
107	6B	,
108	6C	%
109	6D	−
110	6E	>
111	6F	?
112	70	
113	71	
114	72	
115	73	
116	74	
117	75	
118	76	
119	77	
120	78	
121	79	__

122	7A	:
123	7B	£
124	7C	@
125	7D	'
126	7E	=
127	7F	"
128	80	
129	81	a
130	82	b
131	83	c
132	84	d
133	85	e
134	86	f
135	87	g
136	88	h
137	89	i
138	8A	
139	8B	
140	8C	
141	8D	
142	8E	
143	8F	
144	90	
145	91	j
146	92	k
147	93	l
148	94	m
149	95	n
150	96	o
151	97	p
152	98	q
153	99	r
154	9A	
155	9B	
156	9C	
157	9D	
158	9E	
159	9F	
160	A0	
161	A1	
162	A2	s
163	A3	t
164	A4	u
165	A5	v
166	A6	w

167	A7	x
168	A8	y
169	A9	z
170	AA	
171	AB	
172	AC	
173	AD	
174	AE	
175	AF	
176	B0	
177	B1	
178	B2	
179	B3	
180	B4	
181	B5	
182	B6	
183	B7	
184	B8	
185	B9	
186	BA	
187	BB	
188	BC	
189	BD	
190	BE	
191	BF	
192	C0	{
193	C1	A
194	C2	B
195	C3	C
196	C4	D
197	C5	E
198	C6	F
199	C7	G
200	C8	H
201	C9	I
202	CA	
203	CB	
204	CC	
205	CD	
206	CE	
207	CF	
208	D0	¤
209	D1	J
210	D2	K
211	D3	L

212	D4	M
213	D5	N
214	D6	O
215	D7	P
216	D8	Q
217	D9	R
218	DA	
219	DB	
220	DC	
221	DD	
222	DE	
223	DF	
224	E0	\
225	E1	
226	E2	S
227	E3	T
228	E4	U
229	E5	V
230	E6	W
231	E7	X
232	E8	Y
233	E9	Z
234	EA	
235	EB	
236	EC	
237	ED	
238	EE	
239	EF	
240	F0	0
241	F1	1
242	F2	2
243	F3	3
244	F4	4
245	F5	5
246	F6	6
247	F7	7
248	F8	8
249	F9	9
250	FA	:
251	FB	
252	FC	
253	FD	
254	FE	
255	FF	

An Invitation

Sigma Press is still expanding—and not just in computing, for which we are best known. Our marketing is handled by John Wiley and Sons Ltd, the UK subsidiary of a major American publisher. With our speed of publication and Wiley's marketing skills, we can make a great success of your book on both sides of the Atlantic.

Currently, we are looking for new authors to help us to expand into many exciting areas, including:

Laboratory Automation
Communications
Electronics
Professional Computing
New Technology
Personal computing
Artificial Intelligence
General Science
Engineering Applications

If you have a practical turn of mind, combined with a flair for writing, why not put your talents to good use? For further information on how to make a success of your book, write to:

Graham Beech, Editor-in-Chief, Sigma Press,
98a Water Lane, Wilmslow, Cheshire SK9 5BB
or, phone 0625-531035

Other Sigma Press Books

Current prices and further details are to be found in our full catalogue.

Title & Author	Subject	ISBN	Publication Date
CAD on the PC– and Compatibles: H.S. Atherton	How to design and draft reliably with an IBM-PC or compatible. Both 2D drafting and 3D modelling are explained and illustrated with representative software packages	1-85058-089-8	Autumn 1987
Designing Artificial Intelligence Software: A. Bahrami	This provides a collection of AI based programming techniques that can be applied to solving every day programming problems together with descriptions of frontier research.	1-85058-085-5	Winter 1987
Artificial Intelligence–a European Perspective: I. Bratko & N. Lavrac	A collection of papers written by leading European researchers in many areas of AI with an emphasis on machine learning.	1-85058-088-X	Spring 1987
Cost Effective Local Area Networks: S. Bridges	A complete guide to the theory and practice of local area networks.	0-90510-486-2	Published

Title / Author	Description	ISBN	Status
Exploiting MS–DOS (on the Amstrad PC 1512 and all IBM PC Compatibles: *N. J. Backhurst & P. Davies*	This covers all versions of MS-DOS currently in use (including version 3.2 on the Amstrad PC1512), plus a section on MS-DOS Windows and versions 4.0 & 5.0. Suitable for beginners and experienced users.	1-85058-070-7	Autumn 1987
UNIX–The Book: *M. Banahan & A. Rutter*	The title says it all!	0-90510-421-8	Published
Interactive Learning on the IBM PC: *Graham Beech*	Comprehensive guide to the methods and practice of computer assisted and computer-managed learning, with examples for the IBM-PC.	1-85058-057-X	Published
Understanding dBase III & II: *G. Burns*	Packed with tested examples of dBase applications.	0-90510-475-7	Published
Database Applications in Engineering: *G. Burns*	Covers a wide spectrum of applications with solutions in both Lotus and dBase.	1-85058-075-8	Autumn 1987
CP/M : the Software Bus *A. Clarke, J.M. Eaton and D. Powys-Lybbe*	The most popular and authoritative CP/M book in the UK.	0-905104-18-8	Published
Parallel Processing–with Occam: *Alison Carling*	An introduction to parallel concepts for those with some knowledge of computers and computer terminology. No specialist background is necessary.	1-85058-077-4	Summer 1987

Title / Author	Description	ISBN	Status
Expert Systems for Personal Computers: M. Chadwick & J.A. Hannah	Emphasises the development of rule-based systems, written in BASIC or LOGO.	1-85058-044-8	Published
Expert Medical Systems: M.K. Chytil (Ed.)	International collection of papers on this emerging subject.	1-85058-047-2	Spring 1987
Prolog: Programming for Tomorrow: J. Doores, A.R. Reiblein & S. Vadera	Complete tutorial with numerous practical examples. Covers the Edinburgh/ICL dialect.	0-905104-52	Spring 1987
Amstrads & Artificial Intelligence: P.J. Hall	This transfers many classic AI systems to the popular Amstrad CPC range. Readily transferable to other micros.	1-85058-038-3	Published
How to Solve it in LISP: on the IBM PC & Compatibles: P.J. Hall	Emphasises LISP in statistics, general business applications and simulations. Databases and expert systems are also examined.	1-85058-005-7	Summer 1987
Practical C: M. Harrison	Down-to-earth, compact guide to the C language.	1-85058-035-9	Published
A Programmer's Guide to GEM— on the IBM PC & Compatibles: B. Howling & A. Pepper	This is aimed at readers with a reasonable knowledge of high level languages who already understand the basic concepts of GEM.	1-85058-084-7	Winter 1987
Windows on the PC-fundamentals and applications of Microsoft's Windows operating system: J.M. Hughes	John Hughes provides users with an easy-to-understand but comprehensive survey of the Microsoft Windows operating system and compatible applications.	1-85058-082-0	Autumn 1987

The Desktop Publishing Companion: *Graham Jones*	Starts with a discussion of such computers as the Apple Macintosh and IBM PC plus aspects of how to plan a publication including typography, word spacing, selection and the positioning of graphics.	1-85058-078-2	Spring 1987
PICK-Your System: *N. Kitt*	Equally useful to managers and systems analysts requiring background or detailed knowledge of PICK.	1-85058-031-6	Published
Prolog Through Examples: A Practical Programming Guide: *I. Kononenko & N. Lavrac*	Takes a novel approach to the teaching of Prolog, by presenting a series of graded examples, which are solved in Prolog.	1-85058-072-3	Autumn 1987
The SuperCalc SuperBook: *E. Lee*	Officially approved guide to SuperCalc 2,3 and 4. Complementary to the manuals and packed with examples to clarify advanced topics.	1-85058-080-4	Summer 1987
Build Your Own Expert System (2nd Edition for IBM PC and Compatibles): *C. Naylor*	Entertaining view of AI with programs completely re-written and tested for IBM PC, Amstrad PC1512 and compatibles.	1-85058-071-5	Spring 1987
The PC Compendium, Vol. I: *C. Naylor*	A wide ranging collection of 50 articles on how to get more from the IBM PC and compatibles. Covers languages, operating systems, expert systems, obscure bugs and much more.	1-85058-087-1	Summer 1987

Title / Author	Description	ISBN	Status
Interactive Video: *E. Parsloe*	The definitive book on videotape, disc and interfacing to computers. Particularly strong on design techniques.	0-905104-55-2	Published
Microcomputer Speech Synthesis and Recognition: *A.S. Poulton*	Wide ranging survey from biological background to working systems.	0-905104-39-0	Published
Using Locomotive BASIC 2 on the Amstrad PC1512: *R. Ransom*	The only book on the BASIC 2 programming language to be approved by the people who wrote the software—Locomotive.	1-85058-073-1	Published
Expert System Development in Prolog and Turbo Prolog: *P. Smith*	This is a practical book aimed at the development of real systems in the commercial and industrial fields.	1-85058-064-2	Summer 1987
Practical COBOL for Microcomputers: *K. Sullivan:*	COBOL tutorial for beginners with inexpensive micros.	0-905104-60-9	Published
Big Red Book of C: *K. Sullivan*	Comprehensive tutorial on C with many complete listings of programs for business applications.	0-905104-68-4	Published
Operating Systems: *A. Trevennor*	A practical guide to operating systems and how they work, illustrated with DEC systems.	0-906104-66-8	Published

Applied Fourth Generation Languages: *J. Watt*	Introduces 4GLs and shows that the system designer must still use conventional design techniques. Examines potential application areas for 4GLs including sales, distribution, production and finance. Avoid wasting your time with unsuitable software.	1-85058-061-8	Spring 1987
Mastering DOS Plus: *Simon Williams*	Takes the complete beginner (or the seasoned user of other systems) from booting-up to the mouse and WIMP interface and describes each of the commands available.	1-85058-034-0	Published
The Complete FORTH: *A. Winfield*	Long established book for beginners to this exciting language—faster than BASIC, easier than assembler.	0-905104-22-6	Published
Program Design for Knowledge Based Systems: *G. Winstanley*	Although there are many books on the subject of program design using conventional languages such as COBOL, there are very few aimed at designers of AI systems; this book fills the gap, and will enable any AI worker (or persons new to AI) to produce reliable working systems in the shortest possible time, using LISP as the target language.	1-85058-066-9	Summer 1987